CULTURE SHOCK!

France

Sally Adamson Taylor

Graphic Arts Center Publishing Company
Portland, Oregon

Illustrations by TRIGG
Photographs by Sally Taylor and Michele Brothers
Cover photographs by Luca Invernizzi Tettoni

© 1990 Times Editions Pte Ltd

This book is published by special
arrangement with Times Editions Pte Ltd
International Standard Book Number 1-55868-056-X
Library of Congress Catalog Number 90-085619
Graphic Arts Center Publishing Company
P.O. Box 10306 • Portland, Oregon 97210 • (503) 226-2402

Printed in Singapore

CONTENTS

ACKNOWLEDGEMENTS

Like most people of my generation, I started travelling right after my university studies. Since then, I have lived in many cultures and I love my international life, but I admit I suffered my most extreme case of "culture shock" in France. When I set my first naive American Anglo-Saxon foot on a Paris sidewalk in 1970, I was so intimidated by the French *hauteur* that I quickly determined I wanted nothing more to do with that country or those people. Two decades later, I am a Francophile. I cherish my time there. Though I still find Parisians difficult, at times, I am grateful to live among them. As the French say, between hate and love, there is just one step.

Research for this book really began with that first experience, 20 years ago. I have tried to temper my own view with the observations and wisdom of a great many writers, acquaintances and friends. As a result, I'm afraid it is I who have benefited most from this book.

Of the many persons who have given me their support, I would like to thank Sam Abt, Madame Albaugh, Adeline & Renaud de Barry, Barbara Bell, Fiona Beeston, Paul Bertier, Isabelle Bolgert, Rebecca Boone, Michele Brothers, Raymonde Carroll, John & Nona Denis, Ann Gascon, Madame la Comtesse de Gasquet, Franck Gauthey, Ruth & Lew Goldhammer, Kim Guptill, Gus Hawkins, Neil Hollander, Francis Kelsall, Christy Love, Régine Michel, Robert Moran, Ivy & Chandran Nair, Radha Nair, Rod "Barney" Shippey, Janine & Charles Stockton, Ann Taylor (my mother and my first guide in intercultural understanding), Rob & Neil van der Plas, Susan Wagner, Ester Wanning, and the women at W.I.C.E.

Sally Taylor

ACKNOWLEDGMENTS

Sally Taylor

Chapter One

THE GALLIC ROOSTER

"The French constitute the most brilliant and the most dangerous nation in Europe and the best qualified in turn to become an object of admiration, hatred, pity or terror, but never indifference."

—Alexis de Tocqueville

France has peculiarities that can easily frustrate any international visitor. (We will try to use the noun "international", instead of "foreigner", "tourist" or "expatriate" in this book, as our goal is to show that a positive attitude can help overcome, to a great extent, the cultural differences.)

Yes, France has many potential frustrations, but she also offers great pleasures to those who surmount them. This book is designed to help you do that. Thousands of books have been written about all that France has to offer. Here we will concentrate on what the French expect of themselves and what they will expect of you.

The French have a deep sense of democracy. They believe that all people deserve equal consideration, that individual dignity is important. But, like the rest of us, they have strong cultural biases. They will expect you to be the same (you are a human being)... but different (you are not French). It is a precarious path to tread.

HOW THIS BOOK IS ORGANIZED

Because our real purpose in this book is an understanding of the way French people interact, the chapters must be divided between public life and private life. How the French act in public is quite different from the way they behave in private. First, we will take a look at the way the French are perceived elsewhere in the world and then at the French view of foreigners. Since every interaction involves some form of communication, we will also consider the French language in the first chapters of this book. Then we will look at various aspects of the consumer culture of France... public life in terms of what the French consume and how a French person goes about consuming it. Whether it's museums or wine, there are certain forms, certain attitudes you will need to understand, in order to cope comfortably with the French in public life.

Then, we will try to get behind closed doors with a look at home life in France, a world you may not have many chances to see. This section will help prepare you for it, both as a resident and as a guest.

Finally, back to public life, we have two "how-to" sections, dealing with business and the basics of getting things done. Where we've found other books that address these issues in greater detail, we've compiled a Bibliography of further sources. Throughout these chapters, we include cultural perspectives wherever possible.

The back of the book features several appendices: culture shock defined and various sources to help cope with it, the equally difficult task of going home and the Bibliography mentioned above.

This book is only a broad sketch of French culture, but we hope the insights you gain here will bring you more quickly to appreciate those remarkable people, the French...

The First Step: Survival

There are certain basics of cultural survival in any country, like eating, dressing and communicating. In France, each of these is an art form. To be able to communicate basic needs and desires in French will make a tremendous difference in getting you started in France. Most French people are more tolerant of poor French than good English. The section on "Learning French" gives you a starting point with the French language, if you haven't started already. Be patient and don't lose hope, you'll be challenged and rewarded. And you'll find yourself getting plenty of practice. The French love to talk and the art of conversation in France is described in detail.

The dress code in France appears to be typically western, but when in Paris, you'll see that the French have a unique philosophy about what they wear and a specific attitude about the way they look. These you will pick up quickly, just by imitation, but you will get some hints from the section on "Fashion" in the chapter dealing with French society.

Eating. Ah, here is your first reward for coping with the complexities of France. The endless cultural joy and daily concern of the French is the meal. A full two hours is often devoted to the analysis of the food on the plate.

The Next Step: Understanding Cultural Differences

Culture shock can be reduced considerably if you know something of how the French see themselves, both in public and in private life. We start at the bottom with cultural stereotypes, which we hope to avoid elsewhere in this book. Real understanding goes beyond stereotypes; that is the lifelong adventure of the international.

Among the sources for this book, the insights of Raymonde Carroll's book, "Cultural Misunderstandings", have been the biggest inspiration. A French woman-anthropologist married to an American, Dr. Carroll has also developed an excellent approach to avoiding false assumptions when studying cultural attitudes. This is included in the section on "Developing Cultural Awareness".

Cultural analysis is an act of humility, says Dr. Carroll, in which you attempt to forget, for a moment, your own way of seeing and briefly replace it with another way, knowing you can never adopt that other way, only assert its validity. One can live a long time in another culture and never understand it. It is too easy to treat opaque situations as if they were transparent, and thus never really understand them. Like the process of learning another language, cultural understanding is difficult and sometimes painful. But the more you learn, the more perceptive you become.

Raymonde Carroll explains, "… one of the great advantages of cultural analysis, aside from that of expanding our horizons, is that of transforming our cultural misunderstandings from a source of occasionally deep wounds into a fascinating and inexhaustible exploration of the other."

Let's Meet the French

Too often one hears people say that they love France, but hate the French. To them, we offer the retort of American Francophile, Gertrude Stein: "How can foreigners say they like France but not the French? It's the French who made the France they like—and it is the French who keep it that way."

France is the French people. The trick is learning how to relate to them. Everyone with a western education arrives in France armed with a certain knowledge of the government, economics, politics, religion, history and national character of France. All this is part of our universal heritage. But one can quickly learn to resent the French belief in their cultural superiority and their lack of immediate friendliness. This book is a kind of cultural roadmap, examining the various points at which you will first interact with the French, and suggesting ways to make these points of contact positive and enlightening. It is people that make a country.

The French use a rooster as their symbol. This began 2,000 years ago as a play on the Latin word for France, "Gaul", which also means "rooster" in Latin. The French readily admit their tendencies towards self-promotion, to crow like a rooster in the barnyard.

Way back in 1787, Horace Walpole complained of the French "insistent airs of superiority". Every culture considers itself superior to all others. The French are just more assertive about it. And for good reason. For 200 years, all civilized people in the western world spoke and read French. International business and diplomacy were conducted in French until World War I. Consequently, the world used many French ideas and knew the logic of the French language. Though this is no longer true, French art, culture and thought are an inextricable thread throughout Western civilization, a fact not forgotten by the French.

"Foreigners have to remind themselves they are not dealing with a country that really exists... but with a country that most Frenchmen dream still exists," says Luigi Barzini in his book, "The Europeans". "The gap between the two is a large one, but the French indefatigably try to ignore it or forget it."

Charles de Gaulle, leader of the French Resistance during World War II and president of France in the 1960s, expressed the perception that France leads the world down the path of mankind: "*La France est la lumière du monde, son génie est d'illuminier l'Univers.*" (France is the light of the world, her genius lights the universe.) The French love to hear it, and many Francophiles still believe it. Even in 1981, when François Mitterand accepted the job of President, he said, "A just and generous France... can light the path of mankind."

Such confidence is admirable, in light of recent history. This century has not been kind to France. Although a victory, World War I destroyed nearly two million of the brightest and best of the French male population, and the years leading up to World War II did not revive the French economy or her spirit.

By 1939, France had the oldest population in Europe. Her military leaders had led the country through the horrors of World War I and there was little enthusiam among the young people to fight another war. Surrender to the invading Nazi Germans came quickly. Inspite of an active and heroic resistance movement, World War II still lives in the memories of many French people as a time of hopelessness and disgrace under German domination. The four years of Occupation must have seemed like the death knell to French culture, to everything which the French hold dear.

The liberation by the US and British forces in 1944 gave their hope back to the French. Inspite of disastrous wars in Indochina and Algeria, France has recovered both spiritually and economically. Though she is no longer the world leader she once was, she likes to consider herself with a "mission to civilize". As de Gaulle said, the 500-year-old habit of being a world power is hard to break.

Today, the French take the best of their culture as a source of pride and accept the changing world as a challenge. There are 56 million French people, 90% still call themselves Roman Catholic, 80% are christened but only 16% go to church (compared to 40% of the Americans).

The country is only 213,000 square miles (547,000 km^2), but in the Paris area alone, there are 10 million people, including 40% of the 20 – 25 year-olds. The countryside's population density is quite low (101 people per km^2) and elderly. The French identity extends to outposts (former colonies) all over the world. These DOM and TOM regions are legally part of France and their people philosophically French, though they do experience elements of racial discrimination when they come to mother France.

Maintaining a beautiful capital with the highest level of taxation in Europe, France respects a mix of the traditional, the exotic and the latest technological advances. Old Paris is served by the Concorde jet and the high-speed TGV train, both the fastest in the world and both French-made. France was the third country in the world to develop a nuclear bomb and about 65% of her energy needs are supplied by nuclear power plants. Yet Parisians still demand the freshest farm vegetables and purest wines. A constant theme in conversation is the deterioration of the quality of life.

The Regional Diversity

"How can you govern, in peacetime, a people with 365 different cheeses?" de Gaulle was asked. The Frenchman answered, "How can you live in a country without them?"

One of the fascinating inconsistencies of France is her regional diversity. The French love of food and wine reflects their attachment to this diversity. To give a brief idea, we provide a thumbnail sketch of each region in the context for which each is best known by other Frenchmen: the cuisine, including wine.

Only one in two Parisians was born in Paris. Many keep homes, or have family, in the countryside. Inspite of being an urban population, the French retain a love of the land and return regularly to the villages to wander and enjoy themselves, though not to work; a small fraction of the population now feeds the whole.

We focus on the cultural aspects of Paris in this book. This is the part of France most internationals need to know, and Paris is the most complex part of French life. People in the countryside are more friendly and more relaxed. We focus on Paris, yet hope to describe the France Luigi Barzini calls "a unique, lively, inventive, restless, courageous, brilliant and disquieting country".

Note: We will use French 24-hour time and refer to the *arrondisements* of the capital.

Chapter Two

IN A STRANGE LAND

"*Ce qu'il y a de plus étranger en France, pour les Français, c'est la France.*" (What is most foreign in France, for the French, is France.)
—Balzac, "*Modeste Mignon*"

Any person who travels around the world and makes friends with people in other countries quickly learns the pitfalls of cultural stereotypes and cultural generalizations. It is easy but pointless to rage against the "illogical" differences between your logic and someone else's. Conversely, who wants to be "pigeon-holed" as someone "typical" of his own culture? Each of us takes pride in our own individuality, yet all of us are guilty of misjudging others by applying cultural stereotypes.

Though some generalizations are unavoidable in this book, we are going to try to get beyond the most inaccurate ones. Yet there are some elements of truth in any cultural stereotype, some valid reasons why they were formed, even if their conclusions are grossly over-general. Rather than ignoring the monster, let's examine some of the stereotypes now, both the ones people have formed about the French and those the French have formed about others. At the very least, this chapter may help you to understand how people initially respond to you.

Knowing a little bit about how you are being seen helps you understand the person looking at you. But please keep this in mind: stereotypes are, at best, only a place to start on the road to cultural understanding. As you get to know a person, the superficiality of cultural generalities quickly becomes apparent. So, with apologies to every French person I have ever met, here are some of the cultural stereotypes that the rest of the world have formed about the French.

STEREOTYPES ABOUT THE FRENCH

"An Englishman apologizes when you step on his foot. A Frenchman berates you when he steps on yours."

—Mort Rosenblum, "Mission to Civilize"

For centuries, the French have used the symbol of the rooster: not only does he crow loudly and pointlessly, he holds himself aloof from the other animals in the barnyard and considers himself superior to all who neglect to challenge his authority. Many stereotype the Gallic temperament as cold, negative and suspicious, and the French do manage to joke about it. *Le pire est toujours certain* (The worst is always a certainty) is a favorite French expression.

To an enthusiastic American or a polite Asian, the typical French behavior in public, ignoring everyone on the street or in a restaurant, is often interpreted as a personal rebuff. However, it has nothing to do with anyone else. That cool way the French have of dealing with public life is the flip side of their genuine warmth and humor, which is saved for their friends and family (or babies, puppies and kittens). The French do not hate all foreigners. (You will see in the next part of this chapter that they generally prefer people of other nations to their own countrymen.) However, they resist getting involved with strangers, whether French or foreign.

That mask of indifference maintained in public is, in fact, a defense of the private self. This Gallic coolness heats up quickly, especially if a French person senses an insult. This creates another stereotype about the French: that they are argumentative and confrontational. I once saw a very elderly and refined French lady in the *métro* beat a young man with her umbrella while she screamed obscenities at him and accused him of grabbing her purse. In a traffic jam, it won't take long before shouting and fist-waving begin

among the drivers, or towards pedestrians... anyone handy for a verbal confrontation. Yet the French will rarely come to physical blows—remember the rooster...

The French love a quarrel. In Roman times, Tacitus reported that if the Gauls hadn't quarreled so much among themselves, they wouldn't have been defeated. But this quarreling also has a healthy and positive direction to it, which will be discussed in the section on "The Importance of Conversation" in the following chapter.

In general, a French person will strive to maintain his composure, his *amour-propre,* at all costs, especially in public. He will admire you for doing the same, even if he can't. To see the more positive side of this uncontrollable Gallic emotionalism, take a puppy for a walk on any street in Paris and watch the coolest, most elegant Frenchwoman drop to her knees to slobber gurgles of adoration on the animal. Shocking! So don't expect anything less than a full lecture, if you do something (or a French person thinks you did something) wrong. These strong shifts of mood and temper have a wonderful effect in France: they keep everyone from getting bored. More than anything, a Frenchman hates to be bored.

"Flee boredom," advised Coco Chanel. "It's fattening."

"They cannot bear being bored," said Alphonse de Lamartine of his countrymen in 1847. And they rarely are. Nor will you be.

Beyond Gauls & Franks

Because most of the French are conservative stay-at-homes, there are still strong regional differences. Though the ancient peoples of France, Gallic and Frankish, have flocked to the urban centers in recent years, they often visit home and retain their regional characteristics in their cuisine. We will consider them according to gastronomical stereotypes, in the chapter on French regional cooking.

The more recent racial and cultural additions to the make-up of France concern us now. France went out into the world with a "mission to civilize" that started with the Christian Crusades in the

17

Middle Ages. This "civilizing", which continues today, is examined in detail in an excellent book, "Mission to Civilize", by Mort Rosenblum. (All books we mention appear in the Bibliography.) In her history, France has admitted as many immigrants as Australia, and from all parts of the globe. Each culture, of each era, bears a different relationship to the rest.

The French do not like to think of themselves as racist. Tolerance for religious differences was first codified in France by King Henry IV with the Edict of Nantes in 1598. In the following century, though, when colonization began in earnest, the French had to cope with more than religious differences. By the time of the French Revolution, France had her fair share of colonies around the world, and in true democratic spirit, extended the concept of all men born free and equal to them. They were quite shocked, therefore, when many of these colonies chose independence over French citizenship. The Algerian War in the 1960s was a particularly unhappy lesson for France.

Since the beginning of this century, France has lost most of her colonial possessions abroad, leaving small pieces of land scattered around the world that amount to little, in terms of numbers. But true to their democratic principles, the French still extend to these people equal status. Their populations are educated as French citizens, using the same curricula at school, and they can move freely between Europe and their homes (referred to as DOM, *Domaines Outre Mer* and TOM, *Territoires Outre Mer*). Many of these people have chosen to make France their home. North African, Black African, Middle Eastern and Asian peoples in France enjoy all the privileges of French citizenship, but are often hampered by an underlying racial prejudice.

Political immigrants fare far better, as the French take pride in extending asylum to all those whose radical ideas have proved unpopular elsewhere. (France has been described as a conservative country that is tolerant of extremes.) Thus, both the Ayatollah

Khomeini and the Shah of Iran, Ho Chi Mihn and the leader of the Khmers Rouges have called France their home during their respective bouts of unpopularity at home.

Up to 1962, the major foreign presence in France was made up of Italians, followed by Spaniards, though Poles, Russians, Armenians and Hungarians had also come to France in large numbers (over 250,000 of each nationality) during various political upheavals in their own countries in the middle of this century. Many of these people have eventually assimilated into French culture and are not distinguished from ethnic French.

However, racially different French people tend to remain near the bottom of the socio-economic ladder. Since the independence of Algeria, a French colony until 1962, the major foreign residents in France have been semitic Algerians, followed by the Portuguese. Today, 10% of the population of France are Muslims, nearly all of them North Africans. The French refer to all Muslims as "Arabs". The children of these former Algerians and Moroccans, those born in France, are called "Beurs". They are French-speaking and French-educated, but still racially distinguishable and socially separate. They are just beginning to have a political voice.

In Paris, racial minorities tend to group together. The darker, black-haired North Africans cluster in the 11th, 19th and 20th *arrondissements* of Paris, partly by choice, but also for survival. Some French people resent the large numbers of Arabs in France. Especially critical are those who feel they are competing for jobs and paying out of their taxes for the health care, schools and other social services which the state provides every French person, employed or not. Some French people stereotype the Arabs as aggressive and untrustworthy.

Racial animosity is evident in the capital, made worse by the increasing use of drugs and the consequent rise in violent crime... a vicious circle bred of poverty and racism that is as difficult to break here as elsewhere in the world.

People of other former colonies of France, particularly the dark-skinned peoples of West Africa, the West Indies and the South Pacific islands, fare better in France than in many other predominantly white countries. French-speaking blacks are considered gentle, friendly and easy-going by their white compatriots. Many whose homelands have established independence still consider themselves French. Those that are still considered part of the *Domaine* of France include: Guadeloupe, Guyana, Martinique, Reunion, New Caledonia and Polynesia. Because the black-skinned French are from a variety of places and are present in smaller numbers than the North Africans, they cause less resentment. Stereotypically, they are gentle, kind and generous, though not particularly well-suited to aggressive capitalism.

Inspite of racial tensions, you will see many "mixed" couples in France, and children of all racial backgrounds enjoying the public parks and museums together, in general harmony.

French Asians from Vietnam, Cambodia and China are generally considered honest and hardworking and have less difficulty as a race integrating with French culture, as they have a cultural heritage admired by the French.

There is some anti-semitic feeling in France, which may help explain some feelings of racial difference Jewish people may exhibit here, with both pride and defensiveness.

YOUR TURN TO BE STEREOTYPED

The French may have certain, immediate stereotypical reactions to you, based on your foreign origin, or just on the fact that you are a tourist, at least until you can establish yourself as an individual. Being a tourist is the first stereotype you'll want to shake off. Even if your French is good, your accent will quickly pigeon-hole you. To fly this nest, see the next section on non-verbal communication, and from there continue to the one on "Fashion and Style". If you are a French Canadian, you can explain yourself and get a warm, brotherly welcome. Otherwise, don't be surprised to be lumped with others of your homeland and judged by these generalities:

The Americans from the USA

An American from the USA, as opposed to a Canadian, is considered something of a conformist by the French, both in dress and values (tourists in running shoes, blue jeans and a backpack looking for postcards, T-shirts and Benetton stores). They are naive (easy pickpocket victims), very loud in restaurants, and ruthless (power-hungry) in business. Americans seem primarily interested in making money and in how much everything costs. The French are confused by the weak American social ties, so unstructured and haphazard. Black Americans are common in the jazz scene in Paris, and a rarity outside it.

Many French people complain that Americans quickly become boring because they like everything superficially and understand nothing in depth. Enthusiasm is not required behavior in France, as it is in the USA. A Happy Face smile is the mark of an idiot in France. The ability to distinguish and criticize is more valued than being nice. But not being nice, to the Americans, is the equivalent of being rude.

All of us find our fellow-countrymen most painful to watch in foreign countries, so it is difficult for me not to agree with most of the negative stereotypes the French have formed about Americans. Basically the French like Americans. They consider us a bit eccentric, but they think that, deep down, we are good sorts, especially now that the US dollar is weak.

The British & other English-speakers

If you are British, French people may assume you are rather cold, insensitive, perfidious and stingy, with no sense of passion. An English person will invite you to dinner once, then never again. A French person may take a year to invite you, but after that, include you in his circle of friends forever. But since the British cuisine is considered abominable, perhaps that's not so bad. Six million Britons visited France in 1988, while only 2.5 million French visited Britain in the same period.

The Australians must bear the Crocodile Dundee comparison, but they are often confused with loud midwestern Americans. Heavy drinking groups of young Australians win little popularity among the French, who are intolerant of obvious inebriation. The Canadians, with their strong historical connections with France, are slotted as French provincials. The French Canadians are country cousins... taking a lower status rung in Paris, but basically accepted as French, as long as they speak the language.

The Asians

Non-French Asians are generally assumed to be polite, very intelligent, hard-working and non-aggressive, except concerning money matters, just like the French Asians. Yet the Asian habit of keeping one's distance and not showing one's feelings (at least not in ways a French person can understand) is interpreted as being cold and hypocritical. The Asian smile that expresses discomfort and embarrassment is often misinterpreted as ingratiating.

Few French people distinguish among different Asian peoples, even though Vietnam was once a French colony. But there is far more empathy with all Asian and Indian peoples than with Arabs. The French tend to group all "yellow" people together. That Chinese cuisine is one of the world's finest is a great help to Asian internationals in France, even though most Chinese food in France has been adulterated to please the French palate. French writer Paul Morand compared the French and the Chinese in his book, "*Hiver Caraïbe*" at the beginning of this century:

"There is a striking likeness between the Chinese and ourselves, the same passion for economy by making things last, by repairing them endlessly, the same genius for cooking, the same caution and old world courtesy, an inveterate but passive hatred of foreigners, conservatism tempered by social gales, lack of public spirit and the same indestructible vitality of old people who have passed the age of illness. Should we not think that all ancient civilizations have much in common?"

The Japanese

Traditionally, the French have not distinguished the Japanese from other Asians, but this is changing as Japan continues to be a major market for the best French food, wine, fashion, perfume, jewelry and technology. Japanese tourists are an increasing presence in the most elegant shopping districts of Paris.

There is both a fascination and a threat in things Japanese. French intellectuals love Japanese aesthetics: movies, literature and traditional arts, yet the Japanese reputation for copying technology and endlessly taking photographs is suspect. The way they flock to Japanese restaurants in Paris is also curious. However, the Japanese are considered hard-working and dignified, especially in their Gucci shoes and Chanel suits.

In general, the French pay scant attention to other cultures and distinguish little among them. This will work to your advantage. The French judge, and expect to be judged, as individuals. Therefore, we hope that you will consider the views expressed in this chapter as the shallowest part of the book. From here on, we shall try to delve more deeply into the French culture, and get beyond these superficial stereotypes.

Chapter Three

PARLEZ - VOUS FRANÇAIS ?

NON-VERBAL COMMUNICATION

To learn anything about a culture, you have to communicate with those who are within it, and the most basic form of communication is non-verbal. You can get into trouble by miscommunicating or misunderstanding the rules of non-verbal communication in France. So let us introduce some of the basics.

Eye contact

Making eye-contact is a statement of equality in France. As a recognition of the other person's identity, it is considered too personal for use with strangers. If you look directly into a stranger's eyes on the street or in a café, for example, that will be construed as a request for intimacy, a "pick-up" in the American vernacular. But, if sex is uppermost in your mind, see the section on "Sex and Prostitution".

Refusing to make any eye contact, on the other hand, is one way of "putting down" another person, especially if that person is your waiter or shop attendant. To appear amiable, try to establish some brief eye contact, especially with people who are supposed to be helping you. For women, if a stranger on the street stares at you, ignore him. Either don't meet his gaze or stare right through him, as if he were invisible. Even if you are interested, don't look back.

Using French Fingers

When counting in Europe, one starts with the thumb. The index finger and thumb extended together means "two". So putting up an index finger to mean "one" is confusing to French people. Do you mean "one" (the thumb) or "two" (the thumb and index finger)? Don't snap your fingers at a person. It is considered rude.

- One or several fingers circling at the temple means "that guy is crazy" (*dingue*), and it is usually accompanied by a goofy expression.
- Holding one's nose with the fist and faking a turn indicates "that guy is drunk." (*Il est saoul.*)
- Kissing the tips of one's fingers means "delicious", whether it is the food at table or a woman walking down the street.
- Pulling the right cheek downward at the eye, with the right hand means, "I don't believe it." (Lit. *mon oeil* as in "my foot".)
- The circle made with the tip of the thumb and index fingers touching means "excellent", especially if it is accompanied by a pucker of the lips.
- A hand whipped across the forehead or just above the hairline, means "I've had it up to here." (*J'en ai ras-le-bol.*)

French is a lovely language which is full of musicality. But the French people also use their whole body to convey meanings.

- Using the back of the fingers to stroke the right cheek as if it were a beard means *Quelle barbe* or "What a bore."
- Thumbs down means bad. Thumbs up means Super!
- The finger tips rubbed together, with the thumb up, as if one were feeling fabric, means "Expensive."
- The fingers together, all reaching skyward, means "I'm afraid" or "He's afraid." (Lit. "Soft balls, we can feel them.") With the reverse kiss, the "Poof", it is contemptuous.
- That same "Poof" with a hand throwing something over the opposite shoulder means, "It's nothing; I'm above this."
- The fingers flat against the lips with eyes open means, "Oops, I made a mistake."
- Shaking the fingers of the right hand in front of the chest means great surprise and excitement, positive or negative, and is appropriately accompanied by an "Ooh, la, la!"
- Both hands up in front of the chest, palms out, with a shrug means "I don't know."

You will find that the French often speak with their hands. It is a wonderful part of their Mediterranean heritage and a great drama to watch at a café. That's why putting one's hands in one's pockets is considered impolite.

Shaking Hands

The French all shake hands. It's not a strong hand-shake, in the American style, with a long, serious moment of eye contact. Rather, it's a brief holding of the hands with an even briefer visual acknowledgement, but it is most important in French greetings among all acquaintances. Children are taught to do it from the time they can walk. (More intimate women friends and family will do the double cheek kiss, explained below.)

This business of hand-shaking can be most aggravating, especially in offices and banks. I've gone to my bank first thing in the morning and watched an endless round of hand-shake greetings, hoping at some point, in the midst of all this, that the teller waiting on me could free his hands long enough to get on with his job. Each employee, as he or she arrives, makes a hand-shaking round to every other employee, before he or she can really get down to work.

Even in a small office with 20 employees... that's 400 hand-shakes each morning! (That's one reason why they keep the touch light and brief.) This same exercise will then be repeated at the end of the day. Comparing such counterproductive formalities with the rush to serve in places like Hong Kong, one may well wonder how the French have managed to do so well in the world of business.

Don't be in a big hurry, at the bank or the post office, at the beginning or the end of the day. You will become accustomed to the hand-shake and soon be able to imitate the speed and touch and eye-contact required. When you do get into a hand-shaking situation, be sure to include everyone in the room, or if in a restaurant, everyone at the table.

The Double Kiss

Between close acquaintances who are greeting or parting or family members, a kiss on both cheeks is normal, even in public. Don't panic. This is not expected in business between men, only between women, between men and women, or between men who are members of the same family.

For those of us not accustomed to facial contact with any but our most intimate sexual partners, the double kiss will seem awkward at first. I find myself more comfortable with this exercise the longer I stay in France, and have tried to carry the habit home with me, but with limited success. Among women, particularly, it is an enjoyable expression of affection, once the technique is perfected.

One starts with the right cheek, usually. But if the other person seems bound and determined for the left cheek, for heaven's sake, make that one available instead. Otherwise you may smash into each other's mouths, a painful and embarrassingly intimate error.

Most internationals have reduced the intimacy of the double kiss by "kissing the air", instead of actually touching lips to cheek. Given our anatomical design, only one of the two people can actually get his mouth in contact with the check each time, anyway. So most of us let the French friend make that contact, if they choose. Many French recognize this "kissing the air" syndrome now, and will often oblige themselves to it.

Direct contact, lips to cheek, is not required to display affection, but adding extra touches expresses greater affection. Three touches, alternating cheeks each time, is a show of further intimacy and not unusual in Paris. Parisian women will often extend it to four with their women friends, which is gilding the lily a bit, in my opinion.

The Reverse Kiss

The French make a "Poof" sound, at the same time blowing air out of their mouth and protracting their lips. That means "It's nothing", either negative or positive, depending on the situation and context. It's currently a very popular expression.

Other Body Parts

Making a fist with the right hand and stretching out that arm, then "breaking" it at the elbow with the left wrist is equivalent to raising one's middle finger in other places. *Va te faire foutre!* or "Get stuffed!"

Making a fist and shaking it in front of one's chest is used to mean "He's a jerk," and is really an imitation of "jerking off".

Raising the shoulders, the classic French shrug, means "This is ridiculous."

Whole Body Language

French women and men, especially Parisians, have a reputation for being stunningly attractive. I've been amazed to find that, in fact, they aren't really particularly beautiful. Their skin may be poor or their teeth bad. They may look tired in the face and the women may fail to bother with make-up. What gives the French an aura of beauty is the way they carry themselves. They hold their bodies erect, and they are conscious of their arms and legs as extensions of their whole personality. They are like actors, whose bodies convey whatever message is appropriate. The usual message is: "I am amazingly beautiful/attractive."

It doesn't hurt, of course, that Parisians are horrified by the prospect of getting fat, and diet religiously, but few are more than vaguely aware of this powerful performance. All this is part of a child's education, taught at an early age.

An international quickly becomes more conscious, in France, of the way he is dressed and the way his whole body conveys messages. We have a chapter on "Fashion and Style" and its importance in public life, but the whole body language among the French really conveys the elegance of the people. And it can be imitated. I've seen women on the street who looked totally, typically, elegantly French, and found, as I passed them, that they were speaking English with American accents!

(HINT: They did not wear running outfits and they were not carrying backpacks, like so many tourists do.)

The other "whole body" language that the French use is touching. They tend to touch each other, to express friendship, rather than any physical desire. This is reserved for friends, of course, not strangers on the street. If a stranger touches you, it is not meant as a way of making friends. Make eye contact and give a contemptuous "Poof".

NO, THE FRENCH DO NOT SPEAK ENGLISH
Language and the French Personality

"In another language, you not only say things differently, you say different things."

—Joseph Barry, "The People of Paris"

There are so many cultured, civilized things to enjoy in France, yet the French are not always easy to get along with, much less understand. First, few of them are comfortable with English. They discuss things endlessly among themselves, and though they don't always look particularly happy doing it, they keenly enjoy the art of conversation, as we'll see in the next section. Criticism is a way of getting to the heart of the matter, and nothing of significance happens in France without lengthy discussion and deliberation... in French.

The biggest single reason people have negative experiences in France is: they will not or cannot speak the language. Speaking French will be very helpful to you in gaining a French outlook. Muster up your linguistic courage and plunge in. France entertains more first-time, ill-prepared travellers than any other country, and it is a tribute to the true humanitarian spirit of the French that so many confused, rude, loud and lost souls are accommodated. Keep struggling along, in French. Your bad grammar and poor vocabulary will be forgiven more readily than none at all, though perhaps with a dramatic wince of pain from your interlocutor.

Chauvinism towards their own language is still quite strong. Even chauvinism is a French word, taken from the fictitious Napoleonic soldier, M. Chauvin, who didn't understand anything but soldierly devotion to the Cause. To give you an example of this language chauvinism, here is part of the introduction of a French language textbook, published in 1977, revised by a Princeton University professor:

"French is truly the 'international language'. No matter where you go in the world—you can converse with cultured people if you speak French. French is the universal language of translation at the United Nations. It is the only sure means of communication in Europe, the Orient and Africa. It is the recognized medium of diplomatic intercourse. It is the mark of social polish... the language of etiquette in all countries."

—The Cortina Method, "Conversational French in 20 Lessons "

31

The author may be a bit out of date, but most French people would agree with him. Start with simple things: the numbers, polite phrases, and spelling your name in the French alphabet. As you get to know the language better, you will soon find a reality to the French language, separate from your own. Languages are not just a way of speaking, but also a way of thinking. Although sociologists and linguists differ in their opinions about the effects of language on one's perception of reality, the French language is certainly the best key to the French mind. Many comparisons between aspects of English and French reflect basic differences in the Gallic and Anglo-Saxon approaches to life. Whole books have been written on the subject, so we'll just mention a few examples.

The most obvious difference is that French, like other European languages, includes a sexual element missing in English. All French nouns are either masculine or feminine and the articles and adjectives must agree. Though it is impossible to say the language makes the French so conscious of sex in their lives, learning nouns as male and female will help remind you they are. Among major European languages, only English fails to distinguish sexuality in nouns, though the pronouns still continue with it. Asian languages don't differentiate at all.

There are two very different forms of addressing a person in French. The second person singular, *tu/toi*, is reserved for close friends and family members of the same age or younger. *Vous* and its agreeing verb forms are used otherwise. *Vous* is the second person plural, but it is also a more formal second person form. Even in the informal society of today, *vous* is used by hip teenagers speaking to adults. The formality is important.

Madame or *Monsieur* and a person's title, *M. le Directeur* for example, are the proper forms of addressing a business associate. Until you know a person well, use their last name to address them, along with *vous*, of course. *Mademoiselle* is used with girls too young to be reasonably married (Mademoiselle Chanel was an exception). As you become better acquainted, your French friends will ask you to switch to first names, but they will expect you to continue with *vous*. Only much later, when friendships have really developed, should you begin using the *tu/toi* form, and never with your elders or superiors. You can imagine how this regiments relationships, in general, in France and we will cover this subject in greater detail in the section on "Making Friends".

French is also more nominal, while English is more verbal. That means that nouns in French are more important. Nouns categorize things, a favorite aspect of French thinking and conversation. Verbs are more important in English because action is so primary to Anglo-Saxon thinking. The Frenchman will often devise an intricate Grand Plan before he takes action, and it may take him a great deal of ruminating to do it. Talking it all out will be very important, while an Anglo-Saxon is more likely to seize on an idea and charge in, devising his course of action as he goes along.

The direction of action is so important to French, that many French verbs have their direction built in. English tends to tack the direction of the action onto the sentence as an adverb. In English, he goes down the stairs, in French, *il descend l'escalier*. In French you must know your direction before you take action, so you think and talk more before you act.

Getting the Musicality of the Language

You will want to take an intensive course in French, even before you arrive in the country. Even after you get beyond the numbers, polite phrases, and spelling your name in the French alphabet, don't be discouraged if speaking is, at first, much harder than it was in the classroom. You couldn't learn the manner in which French people speak their language from a classroom course. That you will have to learn by imitation of those around you, in the French culture. You have to be in France, or in a French-speaking country, to pick up the musicality of the language.

33

Once you are in France, listen to French radio programs and watch French television. This will greatly help with your comprehension skills. If you do not speak French now, read the section on "Learning French" for some important pointers on attitude and approach. These will save you a great deal of trouble with self-inflicted stumbling blocks.

Faux Amis

There are certain words you will learn early on that are false-friends in French. They do not mean the same thing in French and English, although they are close. Here are a few of them:

adorer	to adore (in French is only the third degree of "to like")
aimer	to love (in French really means "to like")
detester	to detest (really means "to dislike")
brésilien ·	homosexual
car	bus (not automobile)
composter	to validate (not "to compost or shred")
correspondance	to change train lines (as well as to write a letter)
dame âgée	older woman (a term of respect in French)
demander	to ask (not "to demand")
sortie	exit (not "a party")

No matter how good you get, a major stumbling block is the *argot* or slang words that young people think up all the time. Even the books on the subject quickly become obsolete. Spend more time with teenagers. That's the best way to learn "in" (*branché*) French.

THE ART OF CONVERSATION
When Bonjour is Not Enough

"However slight the subject the soul is offered, it tends to enlarge the matter and draw it out to the point where it needs to labor at it with all its force."

—Montaigne, "Essais"

There is an innate restlessness in the French and a love of diversity which are satisfied by lengthy conversation. Whether you are in a café or buying envelopes, expect a good deal of discussion. Be it the weather or politics, contrasts and controversy challenge the French intellect and heighten morale. Yes, the French are argumentative. But an argument has the legal meaning here: it is a point of view presented, not an unpleasant attack. The French are quick to criticise everybody and everything, but that is often only to make an opportunity for discussion, for an exercise in the art of conversation.

People who say the French talk too much are probably the same ones who say the French are cool and uncommunicative: both generalities miss the point. There is a very highly developed art of conversation in France, and that art follows very specific rules. Many of these rules are described by Raymonde Carroll in her book, "Cultural Misunderstandings". In this and the following chapters, we will combine her observations with those of other writers.

Politeness in every culture follows strict patterns. For example, to enter a shop without saying *Bonjour* to the proprietor or clerk would be considered rude by a French person. So would leaving without a *Merci* and *Au revoir*.

Silence can also be a particular kind of politeness. Silence preserves, the French say. It allows polite distance between people in public. Neighbors will respect each others' privacy by maintaining a discreet silence as they wait at the door for the lift. In a train compartment with six seats, silence will be maintained among the passengers. If there is a conversation between friends, it will be conducted as quietly as possible, out of respect for others' privacy.

Silence can also be neutral, and among strangers silence is usually maintained (except when asking directions—see the section on "Giving and Getting Directions".) In line at a store, if the wait is overlong, the French will make body motions indicating their impatience, and they may throw a look of exasperation at other customers, for confirmation of the situation, but they will rarely speak.

35

To smile at someone you don't know (other than a shop assistant) and say "Hello" is considered provocative, not friendly. If a construction worker whistles at you or a stranger asks you for money, your silence keeps the situation neutral.

On the other hand, to pass a friend on the street or to bump into other parents at pick-up time at school, for example, without exchanging a small conversation, would be considered rude. With acquaintances, just *Bonjour* is not enough. A few comments about the weather, politics, any subject of common interest to the two of you—and sensitive to the time limitations of both of you—is expected. The same for exchanging business with a shopkeeper you know well. *Bonjour* is not enough. *Ça va?* at least, should follow.

In a restaurant, by making the appropriate introductory comments to your waiter, asking his advice on the special dishes of the day, explaining your interest in the cuisine, you can quickly establish a rapport that will turn the evening into a pleasurable cultural plunge, with refreshing insights into the people and the cuisine. This is not idle chitchat, but a subtle development of interpersonal relations. Your conversational artistry can change a most sour waiter into a most friendly one, almost immediately. (See the section on "Getting Respect".)

Such small conversations, exchanges in public between yourself and the person with whom you are doing business, reflect on both the status and the humanity of the two of you. Conversation, where appropriate, is a great equalizer. It can neutralize an antagonistic (ie, fearful-of-being-put-down) atmosphere. Your success as a conversant in France can be measured by the harmony you feel at the end of the day.

Starting Conversations with Strangers

Diversity and division create dialogue. People participate in it with sincerity and energy; they look upon conversation as a skill, as an art. Conversation also commits a person to a relationship; it is important. Your French just needs to be good enough to participate. You can get plenty of practice in the art of French conversation, once you've established yourself as an interlocutor. With the proper approach, you'll find plenty of seemingly "noncommunicative" French people happy to talk to you. The French are most at ease when they are in conversation. They want to express their opinions. They just need the opportunity to get started.

We've already explained that French conversation in public among strangers is usually limited to exchanges between customers and shopkeepers. To go into a café and start talking to another customer would be considered an invasion of his or her privacy, or even a proposition. If you are at a bar or in a shop, speak to other customers only after they have been introduced to you through the waiter, bartender or clerk.

If someone is sitting at the table next to you, he may start a conversation going, especially once he realizes you are an international. That's fine. Answer his question, then ask one of your own or give a comment on the food, the weather, politics. The main questions to avoid are: a person's age, how much money they make and what they do for a living. (Americans, please take note: the very "ice-breaker" question used to start conversations in America, "What do you do?" is strictly none-of-your-business in polite conversation in France, even at private parties among friends.)

In fact, it is better not to talk about your personal life at all. So, what are you going to talk about? The French are well-informed about world politics, history and the arts. Your most important preparation as a conversationalist, besides learning the language itself, will be a basic grasp of French history and world politics, art and culture. (We have a Bibliography of recommended reading at the back of the book.)

"How did you vote in the last election?" is a perfectly acceptable question of a stranger. But comments that start with "Being French, of course, you are… " will win few friends. Do you usually like sentences that start, "Being American, you are… " or "Being Chinese, you are… "? The French love to generalize about "the French" because they each see themselves as individuals first, not as French as a whole. They prefer the position of critic, separate from any group identity. But your participation in such conversation should be limited to your own culture's failings. As a visitor in France, it is better to pick on something you know, your own country's messed-up politics, for example.

Whatever you talk about, moderate your voice! Talking at normal volume in a shop or restaurant with friends, the *patron* or anybody else, is considered very rude. Speak softly to keep from invading the privacy of other people in the room. In a small French restaurant, anything approaching normal volume is too loud. The French love to talk, and they are extremely courteous of other people's desire to do so in public places.

One of the things which makes tourists most conspicuous and unattractive in France is the volume of their normal speech. The French speak very softly in confined public places, much lower than when they are at home. Just because you can't understand French well enough to know what they are saying, doesn't mean they aren't disturbed by the volume of your conversation. Moderate your voice, that is the golden rule of conversation in France.

Conversation as a Dance or Drama

"Once you define something, you can no longer discuss it."

—Fernand Braudel, "The Identity of France"

French conversation has elements of dance and drama; it is a form of entertainment. The most popular television program in Paris is "*Apostrophe*", a literary talk show.

Even if you find a French person who speaks English to you, you'll want to know some rules of French conversation. Seek topics that will interest the listener, and keep your commentary lively, animated and brief. Don't turn a question into a lecture, holding the floor. It is rude to the other conversants and it threatens to bore the listeners. Don't take conversation as a chance to unload your personal problems.

Don't even hold on to a single topic too long. Rather, as a question comes up, each person should contribute little snatches of comment, tossing the conversation back and forth, like a ball. If you are asked where you come from, expect to hear something of the other person's background as well, or his experiences in your country. You can reply with a question on an unrelated topic of interest to you: the weather, the state of the City, the food (always a favorite), the political situation somewhere in the world, the mess America is making of things everywhere.

As the ball goes back to the other court, don't listen in dumb silence. Give little sighs or nods of agreement or understanding or consideration to show that, even while the other person is talking, you are participating. There is a special way the French say *Oui*, while sucking air in, that is often used in conversation. It's a part of keeping the game going.

Raymonde Carroll likens French conversation to a spider's web. A good one is made up of many different threads and angles, creating a beautiful and complex shape at its end. It is unnecessary, in fact undesirable, to seek a common point of view with your interlocutor. To distinguish is an intellectual aim. To remark upon similarities is not so useful.

Interruptions are perfectly acceptable in French conversation, and one French conversant need only give the slightest pause for the other to cut in with his response. If you don't give a pause, your French interlocutor will probably break in. That's not being rude, that's being participatory. The rapidity of the interruptions and the volume of the exchange will increase as the conversants get more excited… like a dance that gets faster and faster. A lively conversation is a successful interaction. As intensity builds, punctuations of loud laughter and even explosions of anger may occur. Don't be concerned. All is allowed in the quest for a better understanding of the topics covered and a deeper respect for the intelligence of the individual players involved. A topic may create a frenzy of disagreement, then suddenly the subject will change and the players move on, at a more relaxed pace.

Such dramatic conversations will rarely develop with strangers, although I have been involved in heated debate with people I met on a train or in a café. Most people will stick to topics like shopping or the food, at the beginning.

Animated conversation happens often with friends in restaurants or at a dinner party. You might watch a few of them to see how they play. The original meaning of *converser* in French was "to live with someone". There is a delicious intimacy established with good conversation. You can learn some more of the rules and style of French conversation just by listening to others (once your French is good enough) and imitating them.

Silence Between Friends

As conversation implies a degree of commitment to the other person, the closer you are to another person, the less silent you can be in their presence. Silence between friends implies hostility. Often friends will sit in a car or café together and one will ask questions, not expecting an answer from the other. That is to prevent a silence from developing between them. At that point, the French may seem, to an outsider, to talk too much about nothing. They are merely avoiding the distancing of silence between friends.

Conversational Confrontations with Strangers

Not every conversation with a stranger will start out as polite and friendly banter. Perhaps because it is so awkward to break through that polite barrier of silence, the French have perfected the *engueulade*, an argument common in Paris, which starts for no apparent reason. Here, a negative comment serves to get the conversation started. This is seen by other cultures as creating argument, but in France it is really an excuse for dialogue.

Early in your life in Paris, you may be in a confrontation with a stranger over some minor point: traffic protocol, the place in a queue… any small situational toe-stepping can flare up into a negative verbal exchange in France. When a French person feels insulted or embarrassed, he may respond by criticising the source of that insult. (See the quote in the "Stereotypes" section about the French person who insults you when he steps on your foot.)

There are several reasons why this is often acceptable behavior. First, any recognition of a stranger is a step towards intimacy. The mere fact that the person is taking off his public mask of indifference to get into conversation establishes a kind of concern, almost a form of friendship, on his part. Criticism is more acceptable in France because it allows the other person to give his point of view. Thus, a healthy airing of opinion can be established. Criticising is not the same as insulting.

International journalist Stephen O'Shea gives a hilarious view of the way this unique Parisian attitude is misunderstood:

"Foreigners put out by this [rude] behavior lack sophistication, for they have not realized that showing discourtesy is a Parisian way of paying a compliment. They know nothing of Paris' *code incivil*, the Gallic equivalent of Miss Manners, and its golden rule: the ruder you are to people, the greater value you give to their existence. Thus, Parisians who respect you will shower you with pleasant little incivilities from time to time—but only after you've shown yourself worthy of insult. To attain this status, you must master the art of pointless quarrel, the *engueulade*. Arguing is to the modern Frenchman what thinking was to Descartes, a proof of existence. *Vitupero ergo sum*, I bicker, therefore I am. And the better you bicker the bigger you are."

In the chapter on "Getting Respect", we will discuss how to play the put-down game. For now, there's just one more point to make about the *engueulade*:

If the person giving the criticism is decidedly older than the receiver, there may well be a parent/child relationship at work. Parents often criticise their teenagers without expecting much in the way of results. By criticising other young people, they are thereby taking responsibility for them, breaking the mask of indifference to play a parent role and help guide the young person along. In this case, discussion is not so much expected on your part as a display of appreciation for the older person's concern!

Argument is a game in France and criticism a positive, personal force. To participate, however, you have to learn the language.

LEARNING FRENCH

In French, to learn and to teach are rendered by the same verb, *apprendre*. Children know this difference instinctively, and they have little trouble with it. Though we cannot say that learning French is painless, much work has been done on teaching methods. Summarizing a lifetime in language and linguistics, John Dennis, professor at San Francisco State University, here summarizes his approach to language learning in so far as it relates to French. He gives hope and help to those who find it difficult to learn French.

Au Secours! *(Help!)*

In a well-known American film, a young, cheerful student of about 19 has failed his entrance examinations into a prestigious American university. His exasperated father hires an attractive woman to tutor him, her payment based on his passing the exam. The subject at hand? French grammar.

In the occasional scenes where anything remotely academic occurs, we see the young man stumbling through the present tense of *être*, the verb "to be": "Zhuh swee, too (um) ess, ill (ah) ess—est—et? ell est…" His pronunciation is appalling, but nevermind, we admire his progress… both with French and with the tutor, as romance springs between them and becomes the major part of the film, implying that pillow talk is perhaps the best way to develop a language skill. In the end, the young man passes his exam, his father beams, the tutor is rewarded handsomely and the viewer is left with a variety of misconceptions about the French language and learning a foreign language, in general.

Excusez-moi… *(Excuse me…)*

Here are the various messages that the film presented:
1. French is an inherently difficult language.
2. French grammar is more complex than the grammar of other languages.
3. Success in learning to speak French depends basically on mastery of French grammar.
4. French pronunciation presents problems because the French language has more sounds than other languages have.
5. The methodology of teaching French as a foreign language depends basically on the ability of non-native speakers to memorize and to reproduce exactly.

6. Native speakers of French tend to speak so rapidly that foreigners can't understand them.
7. French is the language of love/diplomacy/logic.

All these ideas are wrong. The only truth about the film is: pillow talk is one way to learn to communicate in any language. If that is not among your options...

Ecoutez-moi *(Listen to me)*

A great deal of your success or failure in learning a foreign language depends on your attitude towards the language and the capabilities you assume for yourself, as a language learner. Let's try to set things straight.

To put it simply, either you take charge of yourself and the language you intend to learn, or it takes charge of you, which means you are overwhelmed and fall back on the excuses exposed above. As adults, we don't have the opportunities that we had as children when we acquired our native language. For the first three years of our life, learning a language was our major activity. Learning another language, later on, is quite a different experience.

When we learned our mother tongue, we had no options. With a new language, we have to have a motive, an answer to the question, "Why do I have to do this?" The answers vary, but one thing is clear: it is most unlikely that the language you begin as an adult will ever approach the dimensions of your native language. This should relieve some of your anxiety and help to simplify your task. Here are some other words of support:

1. No language is inherently difficult. Languages are more or less difficult as foreign languages, depending on the native language(s) of the learner.
2. The same applies to grammar.
3. Learning to speak a foreign language depends primarily on one's desire to speak, then on one's need to say certain things, on one's ability to imitate new or modified sounds with accuracy

45

and on one's choice of vocabulary and structures to present the messages. To put grammar first, is to confuse the grammar of a language—its anatomy, so to speak—with the language itself, which consists of more than grammar (as a person is more than just his anatomy).

4. The other four ideas put forward previously are *bêtise*, either patently untrue or unsound judgements. Subscribing to any of them will inhibit your ability to learn any language.

Montrez-moi *(Show me)*

Without attempting a substantial analysis of the distinctive features of the French language, we can point to certain things that make French seem strange and difficult to learners of French as a foreign language.

The sound system of the French language contains 15 vowels, four of which are nasalized, produced through the nose instead of through the mouth. Of the remaining 11 vowels, three are uncommon in other languages. The "r" sound in French is a distinctive "scrape" and takes a good deal of practice to reproduce accurately.

There is a way of connecting words through linking the last sound of one to the first sound of another: *Il est-t-arrivé*.

There is a practice of stressing the final syllable of words in French: *incroyABLE* instead of inCREDible. And for the literate learner of spoken French, there are more than a few instances of silent letters: *homme, sable, fort, sous, tabac, difficile*. These silences occur in the beginning, middle and end of the words.

The two most common problems cited by learners are these:
• Gender—the use of the articles *le, la,* and *un, une*.
• Complements of verbs—the use of prepositions after verbs: *venir à* or *de, decider à* or *de, promettre à* or *de*.

Verb tense, aspect and mood are also somewhat mystifying, especially the subjunctive.

Vocabulary can be easily sorted out into a list determined by frequency of use, which ranges from high-frequency words such as articles, prepositions and pronouns, to the generic verbs (come, go, wait, buy, think, see, etc.), the generic nouns (numbers, house, market, bread, fruit, meat, etc.) and attributes (left, right, large, small, good, bad, expensive, cheap, etc.)

Learning appropriate cultural behavior (manners, etiquette, politeness) is less likely to be integrated into language learning outside the country where it is spoken. However, when learning French in a country where French is spoken, you have the advantage of cultural behavior, as well. The relationship between what one says and how one says it (intonation of speech and body gesture), where and when one can say it, all should be integrated into any language-learning experience. The culture needs to be learned and understood along with the language.

It is probable and desirable that learners will understand more language than they will produce, and that they will learn things they may not be able to say in polite society, and that certain practices and conventions will puzzle them and confuse them. Such matters are normally found in the course of learning the ways of life of a new language and culture.

Apprenez! *(Learn! Teach yourself!)*

The list of possible obstacles to the learner of French is neither lengthy nor formidable. The French verb *apprendre* can mean both learn and teach. This is not ambiguous but compliementary: teaching and learning are two sides of the same coin. Children know this, without being able to tell us how they know it or what they know. The learning strategies used by children in the first language are both instructive and useful to older learners who are teaching themselves and being taught.

For pronunciation, you will need an excellent model, preferably a native speaker. Not only must your pronunciation be intelligble, it must be accurate 95% of the time!

For grammar and vocabulary, you can be comforted by these figures: you can get by with 50% accuracy in grammar and you can get by with a general vocabulary that comprises 5% of the high frequency words used by native speakers!

Attending classes is the most common way that people learn foreign languages. Classes are structured, they are generally taught by qualified instructors, they are relatively inexpensive and they provide a social setting for the communicative function of language.

And yet, when you ask people how they learned to speak and understand (and perhaps to read and write) a foreign language, the number who learned it in language classes meeting three to five hours a week, is a distinct minority. Most people have other ways of learning, some formal, some informal.

When we say "learn", we need to understand the implications of that word. You can "learn" French sufficiently to survive: to eat, find a hotel room, find the toilet, find the *métro*, add up the restaurant bill, and so on. This kind of learning is *"primi* (from *primitif*) *Français"*. You should be able to learn this type of French fairly quickly, since you are going to ignore 50% of the grammar, acquire only the vocabulary you need and practise your pronunciation. *Primi Français* is limited but functional.

A step beyond that is mini-French, which uses articles and conjugates verbs and adds attributes. It is the French of French children who are learning their language. It contains a considerably larger vocabulary and attempts to observe the speech contours of French statements and questions instead of the hortatory, declamatory production of primi French. Thus one moves from *Pain, s'il vous plaît* to *Je voudrais du pain, s'il vous plaît.*

A tutor who is a native speaker of a foreign language may prove to be a good solution for learners who have gone beyond the practices of the classroom and want to create their own programs. Tutors may be expensive, so you should have compelling reasons for giving up the classroom or self-instruction with good tapes and texts. Tutors who are simply agreeable native speakers will probably not have sufficient experience or skill to satisfy the learner looking for alternative ways of learning.

As television, videotape, videodisk and computers show us the potentialities for language instruction, we may find that public programs and private tutors (for small groups and individuals) will become a dominant mode of learning foreign languages. The early attempts to provide this kind of experience have drawn large audiences but have not been particularly successful or long-lived. However, it is too early to tell.

Envoi *(The Moral of the Story)*

Learning French may not be necessary for people who want to visit France for a short time. The French are beginning to learn English on a broader basis. In 1992, the EEC (CÉE in French)—the European Economic Community of 12 nations—will become a united Europe. The common language of trade will be English. However, nationalities and languages will be retained and one may very well imagine primi-English and mini-English spoken from the Benelux countries to Greece. *Plus ça change, plus c'est la même chose...*

Chapter Four

FRENCH CULTURE AND SOCIETY

ARTS AND THE FRENCH PSYCHE

Art and architecture in any country teach a great deal about what the people value and how they relate to each other. The first thing visitors notice about France is the unique radiating star patterns in the layout of the cities. The countryside is organized this way, too, but Paris is the supreme example. From a dozen streets you can get a view of the Arc de Triomphe, Montmartre or Montparnasse, because these centre points radiate streets out in all directions.

From pre-Roman times, French roads have formed a mosaic of interlocking stars, with large towns in the centre, surrounded by market villages, each a centre for the hamlets clustered around it. Although the Romans attempted to divide Gaul into three parts, you can still see this Gallic star pattern in any train- or road-map. As proof of this pattern, there are 20 major highways leading in and out of Paris.

One result has been a people organized in a unique way. Edward T. Hall in his book, "The Hidden Dimension", talks about the sociopetal or socially-centered aspects of the French. They connect all points and all functions to center points, in geography, society and business.

"It is incredible," Hall says, "how many facets of French life the radiating star pattern touches. It is almost as though the whole culture were set up on a model in which power, influence and control flowed in and out from a series of interlocking centers."

French life revolves around social relations in "a series of radiating networks," says Hall. In a French office, for example, the manager's desk will often be in the middle of the room. He or she is the central figure in a hierarchy that involves many equals working as satellites around a common manager. Rather than a patriarchal pyramid, with all power focused at the top, France can been seen as "a series of radiating networks that build up into a larger and larger center." The only problem with this sort of organization is that it demands you start out in the right direction in the first place, otherwise you get progressively off base. The wrong turn off the Etoile at the Arc de Triomphe, for example, will lead you further and further from your goal. (In a grid pattern, you can move over one street whenever you like.) Thus, before taking any steps, a French person is likely to want a great deal of discussion and consideration of the options. He will be very concerned about the goal towards which he is going as well as the direction. This emphasis on goals is illustrated in other aspects of French life, including the language and politics. Understanding this approach will also be extremely helpful to you in business relationships.

Marvels of classical and modern architecture at the Louvre. The museum houses some of the world's greatest works of art.

French architecture gives many broad illustrations of the French sense of history. Visit Versailles to get a feeling of the power, the richness of what was the culmination of French monarchy. The splendor of this former France lives on in each French heart, if not in world power politics today.

A Short History of French Painting

In the 16th century, the Renaissance began in France from what had started in Italy, with science and the discovery of the rest of the world. This coincided with the development of the printing press in Germany, creating an intellectual explosion all over Europe. Everything was questioned, including God. New ideas in art and architecture were brought from Italy by King François I. He invited such artists as Leonardo da Vinci (who actually died in France), Benvenuto Cellini and Titian. They decorated his new castle at Fontainebleau so magnificently that other wealthy, land-owning gentlemen took up the trend. The chateaux of the Loire valley are the result. In 1546, the new Louvre castle and the Tuileries were begun in Paris.

In the 17th century, Paris became the great capital city of Europe. Under the direction of Cardinal Richelieu, the streets were paved and the Ile St. Louis and Marais developed with magnificent *hôtels*, the city homes of the wealthy. The Luxembourg palace and gardens were completed, the Louvre enlarged and gilded. Simon Vouet, the painter of the day, was followed by his pupils, Le Sueur, Mignard and Charles Lebrun, who did the portraits of the great families during the reign of Louis XIV, the apogee of the French monarchy.

It was this King Louis who built Versailles into a magnificent central point of royal power—economically, socially and physically. Here, he kept his nobles in splendid imprisonment and encouraged their petty infighting and squabbles, to prevent them from gathering force against him at their own estates.

Although the French people later rebelled against this tight control and unfair distribution of wealth, these palaces, at Versailles and in Paris, remain the visible foundations of French potency. In the poor countryside, artists like Georges de la Tour and the Lenain brothers depicted the simple, peasant life of the 17th century. In spite of all the splendor at Paris and Versailles, the French still recognized a nobility in the simple life. That humanism, the foundation of the democratic principles functioning today, is symbolized by the young, bare-chested peasant woman on the paper money and the stamps of France. Fondly known as "Marianne," she has represented France since the French Revolution.

The politics of the 18th century brought the decline of the French monarchy and the arts. Philosophy predominated as the French sought alternatives to a monarchical system. Art became a function of revolutionary thinking. The Bastille prison was torn down by the Revolutionaries and its stones used in the bridge built at the Place de la Concorde. The people could then walk on this symbol of oppression as they crossed the Seine to the steps of the Assemblée Nationale, the legislative assembly established to voice the will of the people.

The 19th Century

When Napoleon came to power in 1799, he also censored art and literature, but encouraged the great flourishing of French public architecture. By the middle of the 19th century, Napoleon's grandson, Louis Napoleon Bonaparte, declared he wanted to be a second Augustus Caesar and make Paris a second Rome. He named Baron Georges Haussmann, the prefect of the Seine, to do it. Haussmann created the Paris we see today, and other cities in France and elsewhere in the world have followed his basic design elements: wide, tree-lined boulevards, underground sewer systems and pure centralized water supplies, large parks, standardized heights of buildings and density limitations. Much of the old Paris was torn down to create this new Paris.

Poverty and crime were problems, even then, and sanitation standards abominable. (Victor Hugo described the old Paris well in "*Les Misérables*".) Haussmann transformed the city, using Napoleon's sketches as his Master Plan, and with the approval and support of the ruler, the whole job took only 20 years. Following these efforts, the people of Paris took over, relishing their parks and architecture, creating an outdoor café life and protecting the Haussmann design. To this day, the city of Paris remains a work of art.

The visual arts flourished in France in the 19th century. There were three schools: the romantic painters such as Delacroix and Gericault, the realism of Ingres and Courbet and the symbolism of Corot, which lead to Impressionism. Monet and Renoir led this new artistic movement, a brave force against the art establishment that started in the 1860s. It is said that the sunlit ripples of the painting "The Seine at La Grenouillère" formed the first Impressionist painting, done in 1869. These two artists developed the full style. Camille Pissarro, Degas and Cézanne soon joined them. The next generation included Georges Seurat and Paul Gauguin. The last exhibit of these Impressionists was in 1886, though their influence continued to spread and they continued to paint and mature. The concept of individuality is an essential element of this art, and individuality remains an essential ingredient of French values.

The 20th Century

France continued to be a center for artistic expression into the 20th century. Henri Matisse, Pablo Picasso (Spanish, but adopted by the

French), Paul Klee (Swiss-German), Georges Braque and many others were highly respected and admired by the French people. Art as well as fashion and interest in interior design were now the darlings of the bourgeoisie and went beyond nationalism. Museums, many of them the *hôtels* (private homes) of the 16th and 17th century wealthy class, refurbished after decades of neglect, began to flourish in Paris. Ironically, French art, the supreme individual expression of universal Truth, quickly became the darling of the wealthy elite. Art is still the culmination of all that civilization aims towards, big money for the buyers and sellers, and an honored, if impoverished, profession. Nothing (save eating, sex and politics) is more sacred to the French middle-class sensitivity. A person who knows nothing of art is considered uncivilized in France, no matter how rich or successful he may be otherwise.

Being seen at and seeing the latest art exhibitions, especially at the opening vernissage, is a top social priority in Paris, though the buyers stretch from New York to Tokyo, and French art today lacks some of its originality and vitality.

Being correctly dressed, following the latest in the international art scene, and patronizing the best restaurants, are all basic ingredients of being *raffiné* in France. Behind this superficial cultural propaganda is a profound appreciation of life as an art form. This is partly why French public life is dynamic, aesthetic and sensual.

GIVING AND GETTING DIRECTIONS AND INFORMATION
Giving and Getting Directions on the Street
"A map without a compass is a useless thing."

—Charles Stockton

One of the first things that will happen to you in France is, you will need directions. Most travellers carry a map, and if you don't speak French, you should carry one, too. If you do speak French, you will find French people endlessly willing to give directions. When a Frenchman gets lost (and many do, especially in Paris) he will be likely to ask you for directions, himself. This will be done with hesitance and apologies for disturbing you (*vous déranger*).

A French person will stop a perfect stranger on the street and ask for advice on where to go, though he wouldn't dream of making small talk with a person waiting in line with him at the grocery store. So this will probably be the first time a French stranger volunteers direct contact with you. It's a bit flustering and exciting, but stay calm and handle this carefully. If you speak French, you now have a chance to participate in your first verbal waltz. Your interlocutor will wait patiently for your answer. If you don't know exactly where he is trying to go, send him off in the right direction and suggest he ask someone at the next intersection. If you are completely in the dark, the best thing is to turn and stop someone else walking by and ask him or her to help you both.

Here is how a French friend describes how she picks someone to ask directions from:

"I ask someone who looks fairly intelligent. Not an old person who probably doesn't leave the area very often and won't be able to organize his thoughts quickly. I look for efficient-looking people, serious people carrying an attache case, for example, and walking briskly. I don't generally ask young people; they might be too shy or too fresh."

When a French person stops to ask you directions, you should feel flattered: he is putting himself at your mercy, making himself vulnerable to you, by asking for your help. He is exhibiting his real faith in you, as a human being. You now hold his trust in your hands. It is your responsibility to either provide the information he needs or find someone else who does. Etiquette demands that you do not leave this stranger until he is on his way, feeling better informed. If you just say you don't know and walk away, you've kicked the poor guy when he's down.

In turn, if you ask directions of a French person, you must give him the courtesy of listening to his whole answer, however long it takes. Give your thanks and head off in the direction he's advised, even if you know his answer was wrong. If you don't, at least start out in the direction advised and continue until your adviser is out of sight; he may well race after you to correct your "error". French people have been known to give the wrong directions rather than shirk the duty of a reply. They are not trying to trick you, but to fulfil the obligation.

I love maps, and often when I am asked directions in Paris, I'll reach for my map, only to find that the French person waiting for my reply has a look of modified horror on his face and is desperately looking around for another stranger to pull into our discussion.

French people prefer to ask a person for information. They don't like referring to maps, guidebooks, train tables, even directions for an appliance they've just bought. There is good reason for this, according to Raymonde Carroll: a map gives a great deal of information that is superfluous. A person, on the other hand, is likely to give only the information needed to solve their specific problem. For the same reason, the information area at a train station will be quite large and usually jammed with people who have taken a number and are waiting patiently for their turn at a window, even though the answer to their question is probably displayed on a time table or found in the *horaire* display racks nearby.

Such faith in human beings and unwillingness to cope with large amounts of superfluous information has created a breed of official French information-givers that can frustrate map lovers like myself. I often feel that people in France are not giving me all the information I need. This is probably my fault, more than theirs.

Getting Information from Official Sources

The way you ask people for information is very important. As an international, speaking poor French, you may convey an attitude, unknowingly, that puts this information-provider on the defensive. Just not understanding your language, and therefore your question, will put him in a difficult, loss-of-face position. You have asked him for help, and yet he doesn't understand what you need. Frustrated, he may become defensive or surly.

Even though they are there to help you, you need to ask for information from a railway and postal worker with the same consideration you would give an innocent stranger on the street. Admit your predicament: you need help. This person, though he is getting paid to do it, is actually doing you a favor. He's putting his own self-esteem on the line, over and over again. He doesn't need to be made to feel that "It's his job." He's a human being, first.

That is part of the reason most French people prefer to go in person to an office to obtain information or clear up a problem, rather than calling. The telephone puts a distance between people that is intimidating and makes people feel unwilling to talk to strangers. At the office, you wait in line, giving the person in authority his due, then you have a chance to establish yourself with the authorities in a proper, human way. By calling in, you are butting in line, bothering the person who must answer the phone, and generally starting off on a very bad foot.

Once you've established a rapport with the person waiting on you, you need to explain clearly how much information you want. Because nobody wants to bother giving you too much information, they will try to give the minimum they think you need. (Admittedly, some will always hope to get rid of you as quickly as possible.) So you must ask all the questions you can, and then assume there are still some options you hadn't considered. For example, if you ask the cost of the train from Paris to Marseille, you will get the full price. To get the reduced price, at the times that qualify for the reduced rate, you must ask for it, specifically. The best thing is to write down all your questions in advance, and have them ready, when your turn comes.

Getting Respect
"You don't have to be nice to be helpful."

—a French waitress

The person serving you in a café or shop may be cool, at first, especially in Paris. This is often misinterpreted as unfriendliness. Sometimes, it is. We have already talked about the value of conversation and discussion in France. The French love to talk, and they don't find arguing rude. It's part of the social exchange.

I've seen an hour's conversation in a bicycle shop on the merits of two different bicycle tires. They seemed to bicker about the silliest details. As I was waiting for the shopkeeper to finish, I had to listen to this, and I became a bit exasperated. Finally, the tire was chosen, purchased and my turn came. The shopkeeper, an Englishman who had lived in France a long time, apologised for keeping me waiting. I couldn't help questioning the practicality of taking such a length of time to sell a single tire. He replied, "I wouldn't want him to buy without considering all the options."

A French shopkeeper or waiter expects you to consider all of the options, but you have to convince him you want his concern and assistance. These won't be awarded to you automatically; nor will all clerks and waiters be prodded into making an effort. In a good restaurant, though, your waiter considers himself a professional. He is proud of the food he offers you and the place where he works, he wants your appreciation, but he isn't going to grovel for it by putting on a Happy Face. To a French person, that would be insincere.

Most menus in France are confusing, even to the French. Part of every respectable waiter's job is to explain them. He wants you to consider all the options and he is willing to serve as your guide, but only if you show him you appreciate what he is trying to do. Establish eye contact with him and ask for a more detailed description of the various dishes. That will usually earn his wholehearted attention, including his own recommendations for that day.

Visitors to Paris, especially those who do not speak any French, often say French waiters are rude. Yet, often what they interpret as rudeness is really that waiter's frustration over having a customer with whom he cannot communicate. If he can't communicate, he can't do his job properly. It is comforting to remember that only a fraction of the French intend to be rude. Most of the time, it is their frustration with the cool beginning of an *engueulade* aborted by the inability to communicate. Learn some French! Then you can joust with them, converse and criticise. It's fun. The French aren't really so dour. They invented the phrase, *joie de vivre*, which even in English means the joy of living life.

Le Fonctionnaire, *Insecurity Breeds Contempt*

There is a certain belligerance, a taciturn tendency among some French people, particularly among government workers (*fonctionnaires*) who deal with the public in Paris. The negative attitude among bureaucrats (post office employees, for example) stems partly from the fact that they have very secure, but low-paying, low-status jobs. They don't have to be nice to anybody. Their job doesn't depend on it, and they get tired of people putting them down.

In the sections on French philosophy and politics we will consider social class structure in France. Class differentiation breeds deep feelings of inferiority. People often try to "out-class" others, as they are unable to move upward in the rigid social system, themselves. Government workers, especially, are subject to a certain amount of "master/slave" role-playing with clients. It takes a very secure person to handle that gracefully, and it takes just a little sensitivity on your part to avoid such posturing. Maintain your dignity and respect his. Your best tool when dealing with government employees is patience. Walk into a post office and tell yourself you have all the time in the world. Treat the person behind the counter as if you do. If he sees you impatiently waiting in line, you've had it.

In general, the ways to get through to people in public life in France are: (1) be patient, gracious and try to establish a point of common identity or agreement or (2) look innocent and lost and appeal to a person's generosity or sense of pity. If neither of these works, just realize there are curmudgeons in every culture.

The "No" Syndrome

Even more insecure than government workers are the lowly shop workers. These people are poorly paid, have very little status or job security. Their resentment can turn into a "put-down" game in a hurry. My favorite is the "No" reflex. In Asia, people say "Yes" first, and think about the question later, more anxious to avoid confrontation than to answer the question.

In France, some people will say "No" even before you finish the question. What they usually mean is, "I don't know, that's not my job," or "I don't understand you," or "I'm busy now." The ideal of "service" doesn't exist in some bureaucracies in France. Here's how to avoid those "No's".

When you go into a shop looking for something in particular, don't ask the bored-looking person sitting behind the cash register. Her job is not to help you find things. She just rings up the charge. There will be someone on the floor more ready to help you.

If you don't know the word in French, look it up in your dictionary and show it to the store clerk. Your pronunciation may throw them off. If you are in a self-help place, just look for it yourself. Finally, if you are really stuck and there is only one person there who has already said "No," remember the chameleon theory. Talk to him or her pleasantly about the weather, how pretty the shop looks, about anything else you might want, then ask your question again. Often, you will get a positive answer this time, and he or she has exactly what you wanted.

Jobs are a reflection of class in France, and everyone is class conscious. Don't go into a self-serve place such as Monoprix expecting a warm welcome and a personal tour through the aisles. If you have tried everything, being friendly, being interested, being grateful, being patient and the waiter or clerk still doesn't respond, your best way to deal with the situation is: ignore it. It's not you, personally, causing this attitude. The French believe that underneath our class and cultural differences we are all humans. It is not you this person finds distasteful, but life itself. Learn how to brush off a short remark or work around a shopkeeper intent on ignoring you, without taking it personally. Also keep in mind that an effusive show of thanks is viewed as excessive and insincere. Cool is real. Nice is phoney.

Real Rudeness

Purposeful rudeness comes mostly from feelings of insecurity. Some French people are defensive because they can't understand you. Some assume, because of their class or status, they must "put you down" first because they are afraid you will put them down. It's a kind of game in France. Insecurity in all of us runs deep; the French show it more often.

No one has done an actual country survey measuring rudeness, but it only takes one or two brusque encounters with a French waiter to make a visitor feel intimidated by the whole country. This spoils things for everyone and makes it hard to stay cool and polite, but this is your first rule.

You can prepare for these rude few in France. Remember, these people don't hate you as an American/British/Asian, in particular.

They are equally, or more, rude to other French people. Here's how you play...

... *The Rudeness Game in France*

The waiter/clerk's position is, "I am feeling (choose any or all) tired/insecure/pressured/bored, and here is this client I have to wait on. Yuk!" You can play one of several positions:

1. You can take it personally, feel "put down" by this person and get resentful. Then, you lose the game.
2. You can play, "You may feel tired/insecure/pressured/bored, but I am here to get a little service, godamit. I can also put YOU down, I want this, this and this." With that, you must snap back with your order, in good French. Usually, the waiter/clerk will stonily fill the order, but he won't get any friendlier. That's a draw. (An unfortunate exchange in my opinion, which requires very good language skills, anyway.) The refusal to make eye contact can become a contest of this sort. I've seen a waiter and a client in a restaurant go through the entire ordering procedure, each diligently avoiding even looking in the other's direction. They managed to do it, so I guess that means they both "won," but what a shallow victory!
3. Your best position is the third one. You play, "I'm not going to be put down by you. I have time and patience and I am going to remain gracious and try to be friendly and ask for your advice and perhaps you will quit this silly game and realize that I am here for a valid reason as you are part of the solution to my problem." Nine times out of ten, you will win if you take this position, even if your French is poor.

Smile, But Avoid a Happy Face

Human beings are chameleons at heart. If you remain gracious, not submissive, but friendly and reasonable, then you will often see that abusive attitude evaporate into your openness reflected back on you... not in a wide, silly grin, but in a relaxation of hostilities. Congratulations! You've really both won!

You won't always win the rudeness game in France. It helps to keep your feathers well-oiled so insults roll off your back. As an international, from the moment you open your mouth, you're vulnerable. Just because you can't return verbal abuse doesn't mean you are helpless. Be polite and see if they don't improve.

You will need to develop a critical eye and watch out for "tricks," especially things like short-changing and over-charging, but don't let this create paranoia. Real rudeness does not happen that often, even in Paris. When it does, there's no reason for you to be stumped.

FASHION AND STYLE
Street Fashion

"The French are full of flattery for themselves," Coco Chanel once said. Some people criticise the French, especially the Parisians, for their overwhelming concern for the way they look. Indeed, there is something of the "peacock" syndrome in Paris. People dress to show off, to display their taste and sense of class. Being well (and expensively) dressed and well-groomed can become a primary occupation, even for the international here, if you want to feel like you are part of the scene.

Yet you can't fail to admire these peacocks. The French are not frivolous about their street clothes. Chanel herself wore her suits seven or eight years (lacking dry cleaners, she then progressed to her line of perfumes). She chose materials that would last for 20 years. "Elegance," she said, "is the contrary of negligence." Today you will still see her little black dress, little black shoes, her classic suits and bobbed haircuts, from Paris to Hong Kong. She even instigated the fashion for a healthy tan!

The Parisians do nothing so well as dress. A woman or man might own only two or three outfits, but they will be the best quality, fit perfectly, and they will always look great in them. Women use scarves and jewelry to make themselves endlessly original and fresh. Men can take a single fabric, a tie, a shirt, and look unique.

One heartening thing about the French sense of fashion is that beauty knows no age. Not only is the youth syndrome less pronounced here, but the whole business of style and elegance is the domain of the experienced.

"You can be irresistible at any age," Chanel said. "You have to replace youth by mystery. Elegance is the prerogative of those who have already taken possession of their future."

I find it incredible, how stunning a French person can be, simply by the way he presents himself to the world. It is a quality above and beyond the Hollywood face and body, or the fashion names you hear bandied about. Even young people in their required denim jeans manage to find ones that fit better and look dressier than those in other parts of the world.

Paris is dressy. You won't find a professional French man or woman in jeans here. Only tourists and store clerks. The French who can manage it will dress in suits and dresses, every day, year around. They wouldn't wear shorts in Paris though they calmly go nude on the beach.

To dress well reflects not the latest trend, but taste and class. B.C.B.G. (*Bon Chic, Bon Genre*) is the term the French use. A great part of the drama of street life in Paris is admiring this continuous fashion spectacle. We discussed how the French effectively vary their bodies in the section on "Nonverbal Communication". They don't slouch, though the young like to imitate the relaxed American look. Parisian women know how to walk with confidence, turn with style, sit and cross their legs provocatively. The men can make smoking a cigarette into a tantalizing gesture. Add to this physical presence and control, a highly refined sense of clothing and style, and you have the secret of the wonderful public display.

To feel at home here, you will want to adjust some of your dress code to the Paris standard. Here are a few hints on how to participate

(Also see the section on "Shopping"):
For women:

Wear dresses or skirts and blouses or well-cut pants (if you are very slim) in dark or neutral colors. Limit bright colors to one item: a scarf, a blouse, a sweater. Wear dress shoes, preferably black, that are not too high so you can walk comfortably. Short suede boots are acceptable in rainy weather. In winter, have a fine wool or leather coat, dark or neutral, to go with everything. Carry a purse big enough for your needs, which closes firmly against pickpockets, but with a stylish cut, never a backpack. Make sure your hair is well groomed. A haircut in Paris is a good way to start.
For men:

Wear good wool or corduroy pants in winter, well cut, with dress shoes. Heavy wooly sweaters under your wool or leather jacket will help keep you warm. A "Macintosh" over everything, and an umbrella, will be useful. Leather mocassins or dress shoes are preferred, though more sporty shoes are acceptable now.

Nudity

Ironically, along with their high sense of fashion, the French also have a notorious lack of modesty: they bathe at public swimming pools and beaches in the nude. Men and women sunbathe along the banks of the Seine in summer, either nude or stripped to the waist. Don't be shocked. Like the Japanese, the French don't recognize the sinful aspect of nudity (though the French also enjoy a contempt for conventional Christian morality by this public display). Join them if you wish, but don't misinterpret such nudity as an invitation for sexual advances. You'll get a sharp rebuff. Nudity in France is another form of fashion.

PETS

Although a visit to any French market is convincing testimony to the love of eating all parts of all animals here, some animals,

especially small dogs and cats, get better treatment than humans from the French. English writer Fay Sharman, whose excellent introduction to "Coping with France" is recommended in the Bibliography, is horrified by this contrast: "The French attitude to animals is a bizarre mix of brutality, indifference and adoration. They think nothing of shooting larks and thrushes or keeping live rabbits horribly cooped up at the market... they are altogether unsqueamish... Yet the French have suddenly become a nation of pet lovers."

Dogs and cats bask in undeserved affection, especially in Paris, where their owners cuddle them shamelessly and strangers will drop to their knees to give them a smooch. On the street, in cafés and in restaurants, nobody seems to mind a yapping miniature poodle though they would be horrified if a human made so much racket. The most obnoxious evidence of their presence, though, is the ubiquitous nuisance on Paris sidewalks. It is a constant complaint of visitors that you can't look up at the architecture, you're so busy looking down to avoid the dog poop.

Pet owners ignore both French "pooper scooper" laws, requiring them to clean up behind their animal, and white dog silhouettes on the side-walk reminding them to bring their dogs to the curb before they relieve themselves. Both pet owners and other Parisians remain oblivious to what little Toto leaves behind in others' paths.

Only the Mayor of Paris seems worried, spending a small fortune on all sorts of special equipment for his men in green in the sanitation department who try nobly to keep up with the problem. In addition to these sidewalk workers, other men in green with enormous trucks collect city garbage every morning, including Sundays, and city gutters are flooded with water in strict schedules to help keep the beloved City of Light clean. No matter. Animals keep the upper hand... er, leg.

The French, whose high taxes are paying for all this clean-up, say it is actually good luck to step in Toto's doodoo... a rather stoic approach to what should be an avoidable nuisance. This is an inconsistency of French life few visitors can understand. The French love some small animals though they eat others; they take tremendous pride in their beautiful Paris, yet they let a poodle use it as a bathroom. What Anglo-Saxon can explain that? You will have to watch your step and walk with agility, in Paris, to avoid good luck.

I believe it has something to do with the Gallic approach to life: Life is hard and cruel, but it can be made to appear beautiful and pleasant by papering over the ugliness. That is why it is important to the French that things look well, regardless of the chaos and deterioration the facade might cover up. Showering attention on a little animal or indulging someone else's affections for them, is one way of sustaining a facade of love and joy in a cold, cruel world. Animals (and children) sustain the heart in ways that adults cannot.

The Mayor of Paris strives to remind owners to "curb" their dogs.

71

POLITICS AND SOCIETY

"...the French seem to abound in contradictions and are not overly disturbed by it. They profess lofty ideals of fraternity and equality, but at times show characteristics of utmost individualism and self-ish materialism. They seem restless, hypercritical of their government and capitalism, yet they are basically conservative."

—Robert T. Moran

From four centuries of literature and philosophy comes the evidence that the French love the idea of self-determination and they are devoted to the concept of the unique individual. Democracy was invented during the French Revolution and upheld, in the modern sense, in France... at least that is the common French view. (The British and American historians will remind you that their democracies came first.) But from there the French begin to part ways among themselves in terms of their opinions on how democracy should be maintained. The range of French political philosophies covers a wide spectrum, helped along by a free press and a love of political discussion...

Mussolini and Hitler agreed that France was ruined by alcohol, syphillis and journalism. There is nothing that the French love to read and talk about so much as politics. France's heroes are its political figures, not its rock stars.

"How bored we would be," Chateaubriand is credited with saying, "if it were not for politics." You will find yourself engaged in political discussions as soon as you step foot on French soil. Your cab driver will rail against the government, the gentleman at the next table at a café will blame the communists and the student in your train compartment will condemn the establishment. Whether or not you speak French, you'll be diving right into politics, yours, France's and everyone else's.

It will help to know something about French politics since World War II (as well as a little history and Napoleonic Code). The older generation has still not recovered from the humiliation of Nazi German occupation during World War II, and though there are many tales of the heroics of the Resistance, most French people do not like to be reminded that one reason they still have their beautiful Paris and the Renaissance cathedrals in the countryside is that they surrendered to the Nazis.

After the American and English forces liberated the French nation, war hero Charles de Gaulle was made premier of a provisional government. In 1946, the Fourth Republic was formed and the industrialization of France began. But the structure proved unstable. There were 22 governments in 12 years. In 1958, de Gaulle led a coup, establishing the Fifth Republic, which gave greater constitutional powers to the president. Inspite of a bitter war in Algeria, he remained popular and the economy thrived.

France still functions under this Fifth Republic, but the echo of the monarchy which ended 200 years ago still pervades the French political power structure. The president lives in the 18th century Elysée palace, home of Madame de Pompadour, two Napoleons and the official residence of the presidents of France since 1873. Social class distinction remains unchanged since the days of the kings.

Though the Communist party in France grew strong in the first decade after the war and the left was politically active in the 1960s, incorporating both the students and the working class unions, the country's leadership remained under "rightist", or capitalist, control. Reflecting this, the presidency passed from de Gaulle to Georges Pompidou to Valérie Giscard d'Estaing.

François Mitterrand, a Socialist, won the election in 1981 by 51% as the right split its votes between the parties of Giscard and Jacques Chirac (the first Mayor of Paris). It was the first time since 1936 that a coalition of centrists, socialists and communists had won a presidential election, and Parisians took to the streets in an all night party, in the spirit of the storming of the Bastille, which began the French Revolution nearly two centuries before.

The French public keeps up with political trends with the help of numerous newspapers and magazines.

Everybody expected big changes in government policy. Some changes came. Mitterrand dissolved the National Assembly and called an election. The result was a socialist landslide. Over half of those newly elected were from the teaching profession, a traditional source of liberal, anti-capitalist thinking.

Not everybody celebrated Mitterrand's victory. The stock-market froze as the players panicked the morning after the National Assembly election. Investors' money poured out of France. Mitterrand maintained the value of the franc as long as possible, hoping confidence would resume, and began fulfilling his election promises: five weeks of paid vacation, a 10% increase in salaries and optional retirement at 60 were among the first new laws passed. These new rights covered every worker in the country.

Mitterrand made one enormous step in 1982 by nationalizing much of the public service sector, including many banks, fuel and power suppliers, steel factories, and some electronics, chemical and telecommunication firms. Many aspects of French industry, particularly banking, had been in the hands of the government since World War II. This latest nationalization, combined with the new Auroux laws, strengthened the powers of the unions in the workplace in these nationalized companies, and gave the workers more control than they had ever known before.

At that time about 20% of French voters still considered themselves communists; they believed in the Marxist philosophy concerning the functioning of business for the benefit of the workers. About 30% of the workforce were in government jobs, at this point.

None of Mitterrand's moves changed the basic power structure of France. The elite graduates of schools such as the *Ecole Nationale d'Administration* (ENA) really run the country. Although admission to this school is by very competitive examination, the bias is in favor of the children of the upper classes. And many of the graduates choose to go into the private sector, though keeping their former classmates as close friends. So, inspite of the new government leadership, the running of both the government and the nationalized companies remained the same.

Up to 1985, the European economy was in crisis and the French franc fell in value. People began to lose faith in the changes the Socialists could effect, and the right better coordinated its leadership. When a municipal election was held in 1983, the right and the left were more evenly represented in the Assembly. Mitterrand compromised.

The French now considered him a "left centrist." In the joke, a left centrist is compared to a radish: red (or communist) on the outside, but white (or capitalist) inside, and, when in sandwiches, is always on the side where the bread is buttered. His wife, Danielle Gouze, the daughter of a school teacher, has inherited a more truly leftist outlook.

By the next parliamentary election in 1986, the right had returned to power in the Assembly, and Mitterrand was forced to "cohabit" as president with Jacques Chirac as prime minister. Chirac was already mayor of Paris (the first because Paris had always been run by the 20 *arrondissement* mayors, before).

A pupil of Georges Pompidou and a man on the right (the RPR), Chirac quickly privatized a number of state-run organizations and the force of the socialist movement seemed doomed. But Mitterrand enjoyed a revenge in the 1988 presidential election, regaining his presidency (he serves a seven year term), and a majority in the Assembly, though he had to join forces with the communists to do so. With a majority in the Assembly, Mitterrand could then choose another socialist (and an ENA graduate), Michel Rocard, as his prime minister.

Rocard was a former rival of Mitterrand, but he knows how to keep his head down. He stopped the brief privatization program and is trying to keep a more socialist balance among the various political party forces. His contacts with the president are made through the secretary-general of the Elysée and the director of the prime minister's cabinet, two government officials who both graduated from ENA.

The new president of the Assembly, Laurent Fabius, is also an ENA graduate, a socialist, and a rival of Rocard. Jacques Chirac was re-elected as Paris' mayor by an overwhelming majority in the 1989 bi-election, and will serve another six year term as Mayor of Paris. By 1989, even the French of Arabic origins found their political voice. And the French were voting for the person rather than for the party.

Still, it will be helpful for you to know the major political parties in France today:

- PS (Socialist Party): United by Mitterand in 1971, now led by Pierre Mauroy. The largest party in the National Assembly, its members include Michel Rocard, Pierre Bérégovoy and Laurent Fabius.
- RPR (*Rassemblement pour la Republique*): The conservative Gaullist party led by Jacques Chirac.
- PC (Communist Party): Only 11% of the voters belong to this party now, when nearly 30% of France was communist in 1946. Led by Georges Marchais, it is still faithful to Moscow.
- UDF (*Union pour la Démocratie Française*): A federation of liberal parties created by former President Giscard d'Estaing and now run by him.
- UDC (*Union du Centre*): A new party formed in 1988 competing with UDF.
- FN (National Front): The right wing organization based in Marseille, anti-immigrant and nationalistic, draws support from both extreme right and extreme left. Jean-Marie Le Pen is the leader.

The legal voting age is 18 in France, and elections are always held on Sundays, with local candidates required to gain 50% of the voting total. With several different party "lists", often a runoff election must be held the subsequent Sunday to get a majority decision. In the second try, various parties will pool their votes to give one candidate a majority, so loyalties must be flexible, compromise inevitable.

Conflict between the parties of the left and right has diminished greatly in this decade. The Mitterrand government has come to look and act, more and more, like a conservative operation. Class differentiation remains and the Communist party holds less than 10% of the electorate now, the least since World War II.

Socialist ideals remain strong in the French mind, though an actual break with capitalism is unlikely and there is less belief in the possibility of radical change. Politics in France is a balance between equality and liberty... opposite ends of the humanitarian scale. Labor strikes, like the transportation strike at the end of 1988, are common. Taking to the streets in organized demonstrations is still an important part of French politics, for all political parties. The French love to demonstrate their political views, individually and in groups. There are extremists, like Le Pen and the National Front, but politics is starting to reflect voters' concern with their individual opportunities rather than the philosophy of any larger community.

This concern for the individual becomes more true as France now leads with Germany in the "one market" plan for Europe in 1992. An idea originally promoted by French leadership, this grand economic plan concerns many of the 56 million people in France, about to be absorbed into a community of 320 million. Many are eager to get beyond the *métro, boulot, dodo* (nine-to-five) syndrome, and most people feel the 1992 alliance, as well as the developing frontiers of the newly-democratized Eastern European countries, will expand their opportunities.

Chapter Five

CONSUMING THE FRENCH WAY

LE CAFÉ

"Paris is the only city I know where you have an absolute desire to go out into the streets, to walk or to drop into a café."

—William Gardner Smith

The café in France is something comparable to the *dim sum* tea house tradition of China, except smokier. Sitting for hours in the teahouse, talking and eating *dim sum* would seem very familiar to the Frenchman, who loves nothing better than sitting, alone or with friends, in a café, especially when the weather is good, outdoors on the sidewalk. Talking politics and watching the world go by (both the pedestrians and the traffic) are the two favorite pastimes in a French café.

Someone once said that in France, one still makes a distinction between the joy of accumulation and the accumulation of joys... and certainly the café is one place for the latter. I often sit for hours in a sidewalk café, with a book or postcards to write, watching the French enjoy a sunny afternoon. Otherwise, inside (though you'll have to endure the cigarette smoke) I get out of the rain and snuggle up to a French newspaper or try eavesdropping on the conversations around me, without concern for the passing time.

No respectable café owner would consider disturbing the peaceful perusals of a client, even one who buys as little as a single *express*. You might also try a *citron pressé*, the freshly squeezed lemon drink to which you add sugar to suit your taste, or any number of non-alcoholic *sirops*, fruit-flavored concentrates diluted with water.

Since the turn of the century, the café has been an important part of social life in France, and you will find the *patron* quite hospitable. Except during the busy lunch hours, he will often engage you in conversation. Other regulars, you'll find, arrive and launch into serious discussion with the *patron* and other friends. One gets the impression that they are quite at home. After a few visits, if your French is good enough, you will begin to feel the same way. (See the "Conversation" section on how to get started.)

You'll find many exceptions, of course, especially where cafés cater to tourists. In Paris, near the Opéra and American Express, along the Champs Elysée (now mostly fast food places), and around the Louvre, the sidewalk café has taken on the ambiance of the clientele. Tourists unsure of themselves sit, stunned to silence or talking loudly to their friends, in languages other than French, about how things are "back home". These cafés have the aura of the "culture shocked", and might well be avoided.

It only takes a little bit of sunshine to get the French out onto the sidewalk for their café or drinks.

Cafés serve simple lunches during the business week, and during that noontime rush, the staff will be too busy feeding great numbers of people to worry about hospitality. In fact, I always find lunch time in Paris a bit challenging. Waiters speak quickly, often too busy to give you a menu or make up the bill (*l'addition*) when you want it. They get orders confused, which are difficult to correct. It's sometimes a challenge to eat at all.

The friendly, relaxed pace will resume after two o'clock. The best time to be at a café is after the noontime rush, when the regulars take over. Children are welcome and can be served alcohol if they are over the age of 14.

The food menu will not be lengthy: *un plat varié* of vegetables in season with a piece of ham, an entrecote steak with *pommes frites*, one or two tarts for dessert. Outside of lunchtime, mainly sandwiches or hot *croque-monsieurs* will be available, along with ice cream and any tarts left over from lunch.

If you are alone and want to practise your French, sit at the bar (*le zinc*, from the days when they were really made of that). Drinks will be a bit cheaper here than at the table. Once at the bar, you should stay there. If you later move to a table, the price of what you bought will go up, automatically. For whatever you order, you will be expected to pay for all you've consumed only when you leave, though the waiter may leave a little slip of paper under your plate to keep track of your *addition*.

There are several varieties on the café theme in France. They each work slightly differently, so here's a general rundown to help you recognize them:

La brasserie will be similar to a café, but larger, with a wider selection of food, usually served all day. This is where to go if you are hungry at 18:00 hours. As it is bigger, it may not be so personable, but the same stay-as-long-as-you-like rule applies. Prices may be a bit higher. *Le bistro(t)* is another version of this; a bit smarter, usually, than a café.

Le bar in France is usually smaller than a café. You pop inside for a quick drink and often stand for service. Excellent for a quick *express*, but not for long, intellectual conversations. The clientele comprises mostly older men, and the conversation will revolve around French sports. Perfect, if you are a football (soccer) fan.

Le wine bar is a new invention in France and limited to Paris and some of the wine country capital cities. The atmosphere is more along the lines of a café, but wines from a specific region will be featured and the food will be a bit fancier: plates of meats and cheeses with fine bread, to complement the wines. Here the interest in wines creates a particularly friendly ambiance in the best café tradition. A wine bar is also an excellent opportunity to learn about the nuances of the many wines of France (see the section on wines).

Le salon de thé is a more feminine version of the café. Sweet pastries and little canapés will be made and sold, usually to take away (few people have time to make their own anymore) or to eat along with the tea, or coffee, or alcoholic beverage. Service usually runs all day, and some expand the menu at lunch time. Conversation is rather more discrete, limited to the intimates at their own table. There will be no bar and little comraderie. I always imagine couples at a *salon de thé* to be clandestine lovers.

Fast food places now abound in France, especially in the Latin Quarter in Paris or wherever students or tourists congregate. Loud and impersonal, like fast food places around the world, they produce a culture shock all their own and I avoid them.

For the more complex subjects of Restaurants and Cuisine, see the following sections.

THE ART OF SHOPPING

There's nothing like shopping in France. The shops of Paris, like those of Tokyo, are designed to seduce you. The displays are so tempting, the arrangements so fresh and the products so unique, you will quickly begin to fall into the old trap of "price is no object".

83

Shopping in the expensive parts of Paris (the 1st, 2nd, 7th, 8th and 16th *arrondisements*) for starters, gives a new meaning to the old term "value for money". The new duotone 10-franc piece may be about the size of an American nickle, but it is worth as much as a British pound... only it doesn't go as far.

There are few bargains in France. You must shop carefully and compare prices. The French shopper has fine-tuned her skills to such a high point that, if I see a crowd of people at a shop or stall, I get in the line. Even if I don't need chocolates or apples or new dinnerware that particular day, I know I'm going to get something rare in France: a bargain. Either that, or they simply sell the best chocolates/apples/dinnerware in Paris and they are having a sale.

The French discriminate both for price and for quality when they shop. Don't be surprised to find a French person recommending only one *pâtisserie* in the neighborhood, when there are four or five of them and they all look and smell equally wonderful to you. Parisians are particularly picky about their food. They moan all the time about the declining quality of baked goods! Many of my friends think nothing of going all the way across Paris for their favorite ice-cream.

But generally, I consider food, wine and housewares a bargain in France. That old French concept of craftsmanship still exists and is reflected well in such products. Shopping half as discriminately as the French, you can still get your money's worth. But you do need to shop around. To get started, refer to such guides as Gault-Millau's Paris Shopping tome, which recommends shops for nearly every kind of product.

The only prices controlled in France are bread and pharmaceuticals. Everything else is free market, and the French take such liberties seriously: so buyer beware. Some products are consistently more expensive in France: electronics (especially everything made in Japan, which is subject to a higher duty than other GATT country imports), cosmetics, books, furniture...

Ordering and Paying

In many shops and in the markets, you will often find a curious French system of paying that seems quite inefficient to many visitors, but is really a reflection of the French ambivalence towards money. You will make your order with one person, who then gives you a ticket or shouts to another person the price of your purchase. You pay that person, the cashier, for your purchase. Even in the modern department stores, this indirect system prevails. The reason for this is to allow the person waiting on you to be more personable, to present the products to you without the unpleasant distraction of an exchange of money. (We'll discuss money in more detail in the business section.) Usually cashiers are more senior than service personnel. Generally they are women and often they are the owners of the shop. Money exchange is a serious and delicate thing, in France, so it is left to those with wisdom and authority.

You will also find evidence of a strong sense of honor in shops. Products are often on display in the streets whenever the weather is good, while the shopkeeper is inside. One could easily lift and take whatever one wanted. Yet, in the flip side of this honesty, is a common short-changing practice. Count your change carefully. It's almost a game, giving incorrect change, and you are considered stupid if you let it happen to you. Also watch for pickpockets on busy streets. Now, on to the variety of shops in France!

Food Shopping—The Outdoor Markets

The open air markets of France are exquisite, and though a dying form of merchandising in the world, they are kept alive here by the vitality of both the products and the people who sell them. Most people opt for the comfort and convenience of indoor department store and supermarket complexes in the international we-have-everything-packaged-up-and-sealed-for-your-protection mold.

Here is how Rudolph Chelminski describes the French antidote to such uniformity, the open market:

85

"These market food-hawkers are a very special race, both the men and the women: hangovers from the Middle Ages who mix commerce, theatre and social commentary in an ongoing chatter that is designed as much to amuse and entertain as to sell. Like *chansonniers*, the best ones can draw crowds when they are performing well. For some curious reason which I have never been able to fathom, the stars of the trade, the ones most thoroughly infected with *joie de vivre* (and, I suspect, *joie de boire*) are invariably the vegetable and fish people. Butchers are vastly more reserved, as befits millionaires, as are the B.O.F. (*beurre-oeufs-fromage*) ladies, silently dignified in their white smocks, and the tripe dealers—the offal organ grinders, as they are known around my house—tend to lurk in the shadows at the back of their sinister shops, amid their treasured collections of ears and snouts and lungs and intestines and pancreases and other unmentionables which the French know how to make edible. When a vegetable man is in good form, his voice and imagination fueled by a few litres of antifreeze, the merits of his radishes, celeries or artichokes become positively epic, possessing every virtue known to humankind and instantly available at a miraculous price, which would be even lower if it were not for those criminals who run the government."

—from "The French at Table"

All over France, and all around Paris, the old "market day" tradition continues. Each neighborhood has a regular *marché* street and each village has a day when the merchants set up in the town square. There are selected days all around Paris when merchants turn regular streets into block-long open-air bazaars. But the most important day is Sunday morning, when every French family shops for the freshest goods for the important noontime Sunday meal.

Shopping in these bazaars is quite different from going to the supermarket, in addition to the commentary explained above. You stand in line and wait for your turn. You don't pick up the products, you ask for a kilo of oranges (everything is metric: kilos and

grammes) and let the merchant pick them out. Some shopkeepers still insist on serving you, picking out the product or produce themselves, but others allow you to fill your plastic bag, directly from the display. Watch what other people do, to find out for sure.

No vendor offers shopping bags. Bring along a big canvas bag, or a string bag, to hold your various items.

Once you become familiar with the way of doing things, you can start comparing the various produce quality and prices, and begin the serious business of bargain hunting along with all the other shoppers. (I tend to cheat and buy where I see the largest number of French women buying.) Price haggling isn't done in these markets, until closing time, usually around 12:30 hours, when the merchants stop for lunch. Then, in order to get rid of perishable produce, they will mark down certain remaining items.

The fishmonger will clean your fish for you, after you have chosen it.

You might read the section on "Getting Respect" to prepare yourself for the occasional put-down, but most of these merchants are professionals, love what they are doing, and have a good sense of humor. It's great fun to enjoy the variety and richness of these open markets, a living testimony to the French appreciation of all the sensual elements of food. So come early, most of them start around 8 am, and linger on.

The Specialty Food Stores

The first one that comes to visitors' minds is the *pâtisserie*, where one finds hot croissants and fresh *brioche* from 7 am, and at tea time, the wide range of French sweets. Lord knows who consumes all of these in Paris. French men and women either have lightning swift metabolisms or buy these things to feed their dogs and cats. The *boulangerie* will specialise in the long *baguettes* of Paris, cooked twice daily and once on Sundays so that no French person has to eat something as awful as day-old bread. The fresh *baguette* is so basic to the French way of life that the price is controlled.

You needn't look hard for a *pâtisserie* or *boulangerie* anywhere in France. You can smell them. If the weather is at all decent, the shopkeepers leave their doors open, cooling the bakery room and sending tempting wafts of fresh bread out to potential customers. Pure seduction... There will often be all sorts of sandwiches, made up in advance, for the waist-watching French at lunchtime. Better buy before 13:00 hours, though, as these shops also close for lunch and some do not reopen in the afternoon.

Next to marvel upon must be the fish (*poissonerie*) and meat (*charcuterie*) shops. Rudolph Chelminski has another wonderfully amusing passage in his book on the *charcuterie* in France:

"... the *charcuteries* rank along with the wheel, gunpowder and Catherine Deneuve as fundamental contributions to civilization. Literally, the word refers back to the cookers of meat—in medieval French, *chaircuitier*—but in modern terms, it has come to mean a very special kind of artisanal food shop halfway between a butcher, where everything is raw, and the grocery store or supermarket, where everything is cooked, canned, conserved and industrially embalmed in one way or another. The *charcutiers* are more cooks than grocers, and what they sell is meant to be taken out and eaten at home or in the office. All of them offer the usual selection of cooked and smoked hams, of course, and sausages and cold cuts and pickles and even some canned and dried goods, but the heart of the *charcuterie* is in the dishes which the *patron* has cooked up fresh for the day: the whole chickens roasting on the *tournebroche* out on the sidewalk; the vats of the peculiarly bland French version of *sauerkraut*; the pork and veal roasts, and the *rosbif* French style, so rare that the middle is hardly cooked at all. Around these staples, artfully arranged in the front window and then behind display counters inside, are several cornucopias of salads, cold omelets, smoked salmon, scallops on the half shell with *béchamel* sauce, decorated with little crescents of *pâte feuilletée*: these and a score of other delicacies, all of them sultry and seductive and ready to go home with the first customer who addresses them a kind word and a small banknote. A *charcutier*'s front window display is enough to make grown men weep with pleasure and anticipation. I always carry a handkerchief myself, just in case."

You probably won't need a hankerchief, but do carry a shopping bag or large purse along for all the goodies they offer. Specialty shops in France do not offer plastic bags. You get those at the supermarkets.

Shopping For Things Other than Food
The big French department stores, Printemps, Galeries Lafayette, Bon Marché and the rest, look very little different from Harrod's in London, Seibu in Tokyo or Saks Fifth Avenue in New York. They carry everything from toys to canned goods, but the specialty is fashion and cosmetics.

FRENCH, ENGLISH AND US CLOTHING SIZES

Women's dresses, knitwear and blouses

F	36	38	40	42	44	46	48
GB	10	12	14	16	18	20	22
USA	8	10	12	14	16	18	20

Women's stockings

F	1	2	3	4	5
USA	$8\frac{1}{2}$	9	$9\frac{1}{2}$	10	$10\frac{1}{2}$

Women's shoes

F	$35\frac{1}{2}$	36	$36\frac{1}{2}$	37	$37\frac{1}{2}$	38	39
GB	3	$3\frac{1}{2}$	4	$4\frac{1}{2}$	5	$5\frac{1}{2}$	6
USA	4	$4\frac{1}{2}$	5	$5\frac{1}{2}$	6	$6\frac{1}{2}$	$7\frac{1}{2}$

Men's shoes

F	39	40	41	42	43	44	45
GB	$5\frac{1}{2}$	$6\frac{1}{2}$	7	8	$8\frac{1}{2}$	$9\frac{1}{2}$	$10\frac{1}{2}$
USA	6	7	$7\frac{1}{2}$	$8\frac{1}{2}$	9	10	11

Men's suits

F	36	38	40	42	44	46	48
GB	35	36	37	38	39	40	42
USA	35	36	37	38	39	40	42

Men's shirts

F	36	37	38	39	40	41	42
USA	14	$14\frac{1}{2}$	15	$15\frac{1}{2}$	16	$16\frac{1}{2}$	17

Men's sweaters

F	36	38	40	42	44	46
GB	46	48	51	54	56	59
USA	46	48	51	54	56	59

The big French department stores cater to visitors, offer money changing services, export discounts, a travel agency and theatre ticket sales. They also boast a well-trained multi-lingual staff. As such, they provide a good place to go to when you want to avoid culture shock.

There are big discount stores in France, which have all the charm of these anonymous inventions found elsewhere in the world. Even the French haven't managed to overcome that problem. But you can find bargains at these which will never be available in the little specialty stores. But even in Monoprix, Prisunic and the rest of them, you have to compare prices.

Shopping for Cultural Specialties

No matter how good you are at coping with another culture, everybody wants to taste something from home, from time to time. Although most international cuisines have been adapted to French tastes, you can find the most authentic ethnic shops in the areas where those people live.

- Arabic food   19th and 20th *arrondissements*
- American food   the General Store in the 7th
- British food   Marks & Spencer near the Opéra
- Chinese food   13th and 19th
- Greek food   in the 5th
- Hebrew food   the Marais, on rue des Rosiers
- Indian food   Gare du Nord area, near rue Faubourg St. Denis
- Italian food   all over town
- Japanese food   near the Opéra, on rue Ste. Anne

RESTAURANTS AND THE FOOD MYSTIQUE

"Anyone with any sensitivity who doesn't want to live in Paris is out of his mind."

—American gourmet Craig Claiborne as quoted by Rudolph
Chelminski in "The French at Table"

The Noontime Meal

Following the sage advice of Richelieu in the 17th century, the most hyperactive Frenchman still spends a good chunk of his day sitting leisurely *à table*. The enjoyment of food and wine pervades all classes in France, and those two hour midday meals are still sacred, hostile waiter/client relations and all.

Consequently, there is not much else you can do in France, from 12:30 to 14:30 hours. Most shops are closed (see the section on "Hours") and everyone flocks to the restaurants.

In the old days, and still so in the countryside, where married women do not work, the midday meal will be served at home. You are really lucky, if you arrive in a small village at noontime, deep in the French countryside. Circle the main square, usually next to the church, you will find one restaurant, at least, serving glorious country cuisine and endless carafes of local wine for a pittance.

Lunch is a three- or four-course meal with wine. This following a croissant or bread & butter breakfast! (Don't ask me how Parisian women stay so slim.) It is a credit, also, to the French constitution that they can still get back to work, after such a noontime extravaganza. Perhaps, with practice, you will learn the secret. I never have. I still need a nap after a typical French midday meal.

But it's worth it. A lovely, almost holiday, mood persists in French restaurants at noontime. And most good places will not open again before 20:00 hours, so you better eat too.

You won't have trouble filling the two hours. Service is purposely leisurely at lunchtime. Hurrying creates indigestion, as we all know, and is uncivilized. There are McDonald's and European fastfood equivalents. There is something called *service rapide* in some cheaper restaurants. But a good French restaurant treats you as a discriminating person and encourages you to be a lingering guest.

The nine-to-five syndrome is changing that. Some places jam you *à l'Américaine*, clearing your table before you finish and giving you the bill before you ask for it. Most un-French, and not the norm.

How To Order a Meal

Your best bet in a good French restaurant is usually the *menu*. A set meal at a set price, usually with two or three choices for every course, it is either written hastily onto a sheet of paper in the real menu, or on a chalk board and displayed around the place. Wine, unless it is the house wine, is not usually included in the price. It is always a great debate, on arrival, sorting out exactly what each course is. In addition to knowing the language, you will need to know the restaurant's own unique dishes and their names. This is part of the game of waiter/customer relations, which you have learned to play in the previous chapter.

Often, I find drinking water along with the meal helps moderate the effect of the wine. But I have virtually given up asking for a carafe of water. If you ask for a brand name of mineral water (Evian, Perrier, Vittel), the waiter will bring it and add it to your bill. If you ask for a *carafe d'eau*, you will probably never see it.

Whether your waiter is friendly or not, watch that you are brought what you ordered. And gently remind him or her, if you do end up with something you didn't want. If the switch is blamed on a supply problem in the kitchen, ask to see the menu again, unless you like what you got in place of what you ordered. Since restaurants in France are small, you can expect them to run out of things, but occasionally, especially in Paris, you'll get a bigger carafe of wine or a more expensive dish, so the waiter can get a bigger *service* tip. His 15% is automatically added to your bill.

Likewise, check the bill for errors. Don't be embarrassed, the French do it too. And fill in the "Total" box on your credit card slip when you sign it.

As a tourist, you will sometimes find yourself seated in a room full of other tourists. This is because foreigners, especially Americans, tend to talk loudly at table and it offends French customers. Try to moderate your voice, whenever you are in a restaurant, out of courtesy to others in a usually crowded space.

You will also find people smoking in restaurants, at the end of their meal. Although this is slowly changing, don't expect a "no smoking" section and don't expect anyone to put his cigarette out for you. Smoking is still not considered a public issue in France.

Things that are rude include bringing your own wine and asking for a doggy bag. If you are staying in a hotel with a restaurant for several days, or you've found a favorite neighborhood spot, you can often buy wines by the bottle and have them hold the unfinished bottle to your next meal.

Digestifs such as brandy will be offered, as well as coffee or tea. A *tisane* is an herbal tea. But all of these will cost extra.

At the end of the meal, you will get an *addition* which will not be brought until it is clear you are ready to leave. To bring it sooner would be impolite. Some cafés leave the bill at your table, from the beginning, tucked under the plate or table cover. They will add to that, as you order, then sum it up when you ask them to.

When you need a bill (*L'addition, s'il vous plaît*) in a restaurant, catch your waiter's eye and raise you arm with the index finger extended, and say *Monsieur* (never *Garçon*) in a cooperative tone. He'll get it. Waiters don't respond favorably to finger snapping and hand clapping. They won't be hailed from across a room until they are ready, so be patient.

Don't stand up and go to the waiter. It's not insulting, it just isn't done. A meal is supposed to be a leisurely thing. The number 1 is often written as an inverted V in French, a bit confusing at first. The 7 is usually crossed. The tip (*service*) will be included at 15% and leaving one to five francs more will indicate especially satisfactory service to your waiter. You don't have to leave anything extra.

Haute Cuisine

In their endless effort to organize and qualify everything, the French have developed complex systems to recognize good, better and best restaurants in France. The oldest and most famous, the Guide Michelin, was started by the tire company of the same name, to encourage motor touring back in the good old days (1933) when few people had automobiles. The Michelin guide comes out every year, giving one, two or three stars to the very best restaurants in France. Only a handful have three stars, and even one star puts the price out of most people's normal range. These restaurants must struggle hard to keep their stars, so you can count on quality, if not value-for-money. Great places to go on an expense account.

The Gault-Millau guides also rate French hotels. Their system is newer and a little more complex, involving a series of one to four chef's hats (*toques*) separating traditional fare (*toques rouges*) from *nouvelle cuisine* (*toques blanches*). There are also the Bottin Gourmand and the Auto Journal guides. Plenty of recommendations to keep you well-fed and impoverished.

FRENCH FILM: C'EST DU CINÉMA.

The French have an idiom, *C'est du cinéma*, which loosely translates into: "It's all a farce," or "It's very unlikely." It's reassuring for us to know that the French distinguish between fantasy and reality, but the idiom is puzzling when one considers the significance of *le cinéma* and *les cinéastes* (film makers) in French society. The French are absolutely gaga about *les films*. Parisians attend a movie at least once a week, though video rentals are decreasing that figure, and both "Pariscope" and "L'Officiel", the competing weekly schedules for Paris films, can be found in nearly everyone's pocket. There's always a wide selection of shows available and English language films are often shown in V.O. (*version originale*) with French subtitles. These can comfort the international visitor enormously.

Film, like gastronomy, is a highly serious matter. The *cinéastes* work with natural ingredients: people, places, feelings, things, colors, textures... to create a grand artifice, which the French consume as if it were as real as pastry, as tangible as life.

Picasso warned us: "All art is a lie." Two dimensions pretending to be three. *C'est du cinéma*, the idiom admonishes us. Yet we are hooked on another kind of reality... somehow literal and solid, and for a time, closer to us than the actual world. Yet there is something distinctly French about French films. They differ in their rhetoric (the design and strategy of their presentation), in their language of course, in their direction, in their evident intention, and in their attention to certain topics and themes, whose distinctive features French *cinéastes* develop in special ways.

Take this actual story that ran in newspapers around the world in April 1989:

FRENCH SHUT DOWN PRO-AM BROTHEL
by Gerard Bon, Reuters

Paris—A brothel employing bored housewives, well-paid business-women and a 73-year-old grandmother has been busted in a respectable Paris neighborhood.

The brothel keeper, "Madame Marcelle", is a 65 year-old woman seeking distraction after the death of her husband, Vice Squad Inspector Jean-Pierre Gambini said.

He said her 20 or so prostitutes were mainly highly respectable women who charged US$100, a fraction of the going rate, for their favors in Madame Marcelle's apartment in central Paris.

"They were all thoroughly bourgeois girls working for 300 francs who couldn't care less about the money," said another of the investigators involved in a month-long stakeout of the brothel. Madame Marcelle received another 300 francs.

Her employees included a doctor, a bank clerk and a diplomat's wife, who had turned to prostitution through boredom, a desire to fulfil sexual fantasies or just to earn some pocket money.

The only professional among the 20 prostitutes was 73-year-old Huguette, who had set up her own brothel 30 years ago and had been arrested then. She told police she had joined the Paris brothel out of nostalgia for her old job.

"She's intelligent, well-educated and kind," one officer said.

Few of Madame Marcelle's neighbors had any idea that she was running a brothel from her three-bedroom apartment and expressed sympathy for her.

"She wasn't hurting anybody. It was a sort of public service. If you could have seen some of the men going up to her place, real antiques... I say bravo to Madame Marcelle and her little girls," said one neighbor.

Store owners in the same street said it was ridiculous that her brothel should be closed down while hundreds of prostitutes ply their trade openly in other parts of the city.

Is this the stuff of which movies can be made? Probably not in India. Surely not in China or the Soviet Union, where such a story would arouse moral indignation. British film makers would make it a study in eccentricity: the brothel-keeper who used her profits to play the stock market so that she could make large donations to the Salvation Army. Such a scenario would be a latter-day version of G.B. Shaw's play "Major Barbara".

An American film maker would make it either: (1) a rollicking, vulgar musical, (2) a murky study of the motives for turning to paid sex or (3) a period piece on a jolly whore house in Alaska in 1906 featuring a public-spirited madam fighting for survival against the local bluestockings.

An Italian might treat the story satirically, as the kind of mess everyone in society wants to avoid. A deft and amusing solution would be mediated by a charming, wise old priest and agreed to by the madam and by the representatives of the government.

Now, if a French film maker were to use this story, the attitudes expressed in the film would already be evident in the responses of Madame Marcelle's real-life neighbors: the brothel is a sort of public service that isn't hurting anybody. The strategy of the film would be one of the favorite themes in all French film: the faces of love, the discreet charms of sin or just love and sex. The premise: everyone, especially the elderly, the lonely and the poor, needs love, both physical and spiritual.

Madame Marcelle, who feeds scores of neighborhood cats and pigeons and who goes to early morning mass seven days a week, provides this service to a variety of people: her "daughters" and their companions and friends. Madame Marcelle (65) and her old friend Huguette (73) are a wily and witty pair. They provide comic dialogue and they defeat the attempts of the local magistrate to close down their "home" for emotionally needy "friends of the family".

In sum, the French version would make a gentle, human comedy out of the problem of the neighborhood brothel and its inhabitants in conflict with law and order. The film would reflect the French disdain for the moralistic, as distinguished from the moral, as well as a dislike of pompous piety. There is a long French tradition of turning something immoral into a comic and instructive study of the complexities of sin and the charms and delights of some kinds of human folly.

The fashion in which this film would be realized today depends to a great extent on the director. There is a tradition of the film director as *auteur* (author) in France. His signature on a film is like no one else's. If Truffaut were to direct this film, we would expect to experience the loneliness and frustration of those lives. Truffaut once said, "Once a picture is finished, I realize it is sadder than I meant it to be…" His would be a tender film, moving easily from intimacy to bureaucracy, lingering on the oddity and fragility of life and ending not entirely happily.

Another director, Claire Denis, whose film *"Chocolat"* has been highly praised, has been making small, personal French films for 20 years. She was asked whether or not she wanted to do a big-budget, mass audience film. She replied, "Why not? But the danger, of course, is that you lose your autonomy. We too often associate the world of film with the world of success. But film should also be allowed to be part of the larger itinerary, part of the personal quest. There is where you find the roots of what's truly original."

In France, *C'est du cinéma*, indeed!

SEX AND PROSTITUTION

Sex outside the family, lovers and mistresses, exists in France, as in most places in the world, but here it seems to be rarely a source of political embarrassment. Polygamy is the opposite of monotony, goes the French saying, and monotony is to be avoided at all costs, as we know. Families are strong institutions in France, part of the Roman Catholic structure, and a bit of infidelity is hardly enough to cause a marriage to break. Unlike in the Protestant West, marriage in France includes fewer expectations of the two partners, but survives better. Sex is a constant source of entertainment to the French, and their fascination with it is apparent everywhere. Prostitution wasn't declared illegal until 1946, just when women got the vote!

Prostitution

This is a difficult section for even a "liberated" woman to research, but a wide variety of sexual tastes are exploited (and I assume, satisfied) in Paris. I suppose one should expect it, given the wide ranging cuisine... In fact, the French don't make a clear distinction between food and sex. A major resource on this subject, a book called "*Paris La Nuit Sexy*", devotes most of its pages to descriptions of the restaurants in town.

Certainly, if you aren't interested in the subject of this chapter, you can avoid it. Nobody is going to force you into action. The French have a consuming interest in the idea of sexuality, but most of it is just look-see material. The big reviews, the *Grands Spectacles* at the Lido, Crazy Horse Saloon, the Moulin Rouge and the Paradis Latin are designed for wowing tourist groups from Birmingham, Hokkaido and Iowa. You won't find them shocking. You might not even be titillated. There are erotic shows like Théâtre des 2 Boules and Théâtre Saint-Denis and a chain of peep-shows around Paris designed for that.

Homosexuality is called "the English vice" in France, but there are lots of variations on the theme. The most discrete, anonymous way of participating is to tap into the *Minitel*, the French computer that comes free with telephone service. The *Minitel* was introduced in France in the mid-80s as an electronic telephone directory. But it became a raging success when "dating services" were introduced. You can now call into the service (3615), connect your *Minitel*, then tap a code (try AC1, there are dozens) and someone on the other side starts answering or asking questions on your screen. You can type replies as you like (there are even English language ones) because nobody knows who or what you are. Totally anonymous. Perfect for fantacising, and you pay via your telephone bill.

The next step up, in terms of active participation, is the erotic telephone numbers. For these you'll need a bit more French, and I'm not sure how you pay.

Then there are the public bars, discotheques and dance halls. Some of these are specialized: gay or lesbian sex, couples exchanges, even "S&M" (sadism and masochism) are available. So be sure you read the ads carefully and your tastes are being matched. These are usually "pick-up" places, and to do so, read the section on "Non-verbal communication" and do the reverse of what is recommended there.

More intimate still are the clubs (*clubs de rencontres*) and the saunas which open from 22:00 hours to 7:00 hours, where your participation will be expected. There are also "women at home" you can call directly. The *Minitel* access number or the book mentioned in the first paragraph, will give you a directory of them. Thanks to the liberated French telephone company (run by the Government) you can let your fingers do the walking...

Where you shouldn't walk, especially at night, is in the stunning old Bois de Boulogne, the immense woods on the western edge of Paris. This is where the weirdest action is. Fortunately for the families who would also like to enjoy this park, most of the sexual action is limited to specific areas at specific times. But you should avoid walking off into the woods around the Lac Inférieur in the early evening, even in summer when it is light until 22:00 hours. The woods are literally littered with action.

There are many other locations for good old, straight-forward, pay-as-you-go prostitution in Paris, where there are said to be 20,000 full-time prostitutes and another 60,000 working part-time. (I don't know how they conduct the census.) Basic price is 100 FF a throw, (plus the hotel, if you're not in the Bois). The basic locations are fairly obvious: the train stations of Montparnasse, Gare du Nord and

Gare de l'Est, Pigalle and the Boulevard Clichy (both straight and gay) and around Les Halles.

For rock-bottom prices, try Porte de la Chapelle in the *10ème*, rue Chalon in the *12ème* and rue Houdon in the *18ème*. But be warned: you get what you pay for.

Higher prices and better quality can be found at the Pyramides *métro* (and nearby rue Sainte Anne for gays) and at the Avenue de la Grande Armée and Porte Maillot, not far from the Bois. Here prices jump to 150 – 300 FF. The Saint-Germain-des-Prés area in the *6ème* is mostly for gay services. Even in Paris, there are still few opportunities for straight women to buy men's services... obviously not much of a demand.

Chapter Six

FOOD AND WINE

CUISINE & CHARACTER BY REGION

"Tell me what you eat, and I'll tell you what you are."
—Brillat-Savarin in the 18th century

Nothing expresses the diversity of the French better than their regional cuisine and wines. I doubt any Frenchman would protest being "pigeon-holed" by his best local fare, so I have taken the liberty of stereotyping the regional personalities by describing some of their culinary specialties and relating those to local character. This should be a fun way to help you learn some of the differences.

(My apologies, of course, for the gross oversimplifications and overstretched parallels. Kindly remember that the French honor, above all, their individuality.)

Were It Not For Good Food, Who Would Travel?

Whether you are doing business in France or just touring, learn something of the culinary details of the region you are visiting. Nothing holds the interest of the French better than the subject of food and wine, unless it is sex and politics. Knowing a bit about the regional cuisine will add to your appreciation of the meals and help you join in with the company you are keeping.

In the provinces, the family gets together regularly for major feasts: birthdays, weddings, baptisms, confirmations and holidays all demand a massive turnout and everyone will eat and drink his fill. There may be a hundred people at table and you may be invited along. The menu will include regional and seasonal specialties along with copious quantities of local wines. Often, at the end of the meal, especially among working class families, the diners will tumble spontaneously into bawdy singalongs or poetry recitals. If you haven't been drinking, such excellent drama may lose something in the translation.

Cuisine 101

Learning more about the endless variety of the French cuisines is a wise investment in the best that France has to offer. We cannot even scratch the surface here. For further reading I heartily recommend Anne Willan's classic, "French Regional Cuisine", my favorite source. (See "Bibliography".)

AOC

French law has strictly governed the quality of French food and wine since the time of Napoleon. The national system of *Appellation d'Origine Contrôlée* (AOC) recognizes wines, spirits, butter, cheese, poultry, fruit and vegetables which have certain qualities dependent on their origins and the way they are produced. When you see the "AOC" label on an item of food or a wine in France, you can be confident that what you are buying possesses the required qualities and that you are getting the real thing. The laws governing the production of these goods are more strict than anywhere else in Europe, or in the world.

In wines, for example, not only the specific acreage, but the number of vines per hectare (two acres) and the way the vines can be pruned is legislated and strictly enforced. The French place great value on their local cultural traditions, and their affection for them remains strong today, inspite of the invasion of McDonald's and Levi's. Thus, we can look at regional wines and cuisine as expressions of the personalities of their creators.

The French at table. Though space is restricted, privacy between tables is respected with lowered voices.

FRANCE

NORTH-
PAS-DE-CALAIS

HIGH-
NORMANDY

PICARDY

Caen •

LOW-
NORMANDY

PARIS•
ILE-DE-
FRANCE

LORRAINE

• Strasbourg

CHAMPAGNE-
ARDENNE

ALSACE

BRITTANY

LOIRE
VALLEY

Saumur •

CENTER

Dijon •

FRANCHE-
COMTE

BURGUNDY

Châteauroux
•

Poitiers •

La Rochelle •

POITOU-
CHARENTES

LIMOUSIN

• Limoges

• Lyon

Cognac •

AUVERGNE

RHONE-
ALPS

• Bordeaux

AQUITAINE

Agen •

MIDI-
PYRENEES

PROVENCE-
ALPS-
COTE-D'AZUR

• MONACO

Nice

Toulouse •

LANGUEDOC-
ROUSSILLON

Toulon

Normandy

Along the coast closest to England, the Norman countryside offers simple country fare quite similar to that of England, with an emphasis on pork and potatoes, creams and pastries. It's no wonder the Norman people are round and jolly. Indeed, they will remind you more of the English, with whom they have shared a common ancestry, since the Norman Conquests of 1066.

The rivers produce trout and the sea gives shellfish and saltwater fish, but like the famous soft cheeses of this region, Camembert, Pont-l'Evêque, Neufchatel and Livarot, much of the production is sold in Paris or abroad.

The spirit (*eau-de-vie*) of the region, Calvados, is distilled from the popular local apple cider. Benedictine also comes from this area, its flavor created from herbs found along the Norman coast, not from apples.

Apple pie is the favorite dessert. With a dollop of *crème fraîche*, the French cultured cream, it's enough to die for.

Brittany

Just below Normandy, the Breton region is most famous for its *crêpes*. The local grains did not lend themselves to breadmaking, and *crêpes* became the staple, used in everything from a main course to dessert. The Breton language, which is still spoken, is related to Cornish and Welsh, and like those people, the Bretons are an independent and self-sufficient lot.

The famous French cartoon strip, Asterix, is about the misadventures of some Bretons of the Druid era, when fighting and eating wild boar were the two main activities. These people have only recently been considered out of the stone age. This is also the land of the artichoke and the cauliflower, rugged individuals of the vegetable family.

The fine white wine of Nantes, in the south of Brittany, has a bone-dry simplicity that has endeared it to the world of wine lovers.

Not fancy, but clean and honest. The *béarnaise* sauce, named for a town in Brittany, is just Muscadet, vinegar and shallots reduced together with butter whipped in. The *quatre-quarts* cake, made from equal portions of flour, butter, sugar and eggs, is similar to the American pound cake. Solid stuff.

The Loire Valley

The Loire Valley boasts what is considered to be the purest, unaccented French and is considered a cradle of French culture. Ironically, having so many of the royalty housed there over the centuries in their magnificent palaces has helped create the simple but very sophisticated cuisine. The fresh fish, vegetables and fruits of the rich Loire Valley are cooked to perfection, but their natural character never altered. Nothing heavy about the Loire wines and cuisine.

Food writer Anne Willan explains that King Charles VIII introduced Italian vegetables to his *château* at Amboise at the end of the 15th century. These included lettuce, artichokes and green peas, formerly unknown in France. The white asparagus, so popular in spring here, never see the sun. Among fruits are plums, apples, apricots, melons, peaches and pears. From these come fruit *pâtés* in winter and fresh tarts and custard cakes in summer. Plums were brought from Damascus during the first crusade and they thrived in this region.

The wines of the region vary from the crisp, clean and dry Muscadet of Nantes to the sophisticated, slightly sparkling Saumur, the tart red Touraines and the petillant Vouvray. The character persevering here in both cuisine and character, is a lightness and subtle sophistication unlike the heavier, creamy people of Brittany.

Cointreau, the famous liqueur of Anjou, gets its flavor from orange peel. The cheeses here are Saint Paulin and baby Gouda, mild and firm, as are the goat's milk cheeses like Valençay and Sainte Maure. *Charcuteries* abound, especially game *pâté* and *rillettes*, cooked meat mixed with *pâté*.

Ile de France (The Paris Area)

The area around Paris, for about 50 miles in any direction, holds 20% of the country's population and the vast majority of its foreign tourists. This is a pity, since they miss the wonderful splendor of regional cuisines. But they miss none of the raw produce.

"Paris has in abundance everything that could be desired," wrote Jerome Lippomano in 1577 (quoted by Rudolph Chelminski). "Merchandise flows in from every country. Provisions are brought in by the Seine from Picardy, from Auvergne, from Burgundy, from Champagne and from Normandy. Thus, although the population is innumerable, nothing is ever lacking. Everything seems to fall from the sky."

Now French cuisine and produce literally go up into the sky. The former market gardens around Paris have become suburban communities, so the food sources of all France now convene at the ultramodern wholesale market at Rungis, just south of Paris. From Rungis much of it goes to nearby Orly airport, to satisfy the world's taste for French gourmet foods. From New York to Hong Kong, restaurateurs call in their next day's order of wild strawberries, mushrooms, endive, whatever is in season, and it is flown, that night, from Rungis.

Though Paris itself is not the culinary center of France, the Ile de France is known for its soft cheese, the Brie, as well as fancy pastries, potatoes and endive.

The *baguettes* and croissants that make Paris so sweet smelling, are a regional specialty, as are *béchamel*, *espagnole* and *hollandaise* sauces. But just as common, now, are *sauerkraut* and *couscous*.

Ironically, Paris is a collection of regional foods, but not of the regional cuisines, which have been adapted (with a compromise of integrity, however) to local tastes. To really understand the regional variety, both of the foods and the wines, in truth, one must go around the country.

Champagne and the North

The world's most famous sparkling wine comes from chalk hills 100 miles northeast of Paris. This region also produces wonderful sweet pastries that go along with the wine and come from the local sugar beet production. Verdun *dragées,* or sugar-coated sweetmeats, have been famous since the 13th century. The Flemish influence is also evident.

Also popular in the north are root vegetables: carrots, potatoes, onions elevated to masterful perfection in a *pot-au-feu*. The local cabbage is also elevated into elegant soups, braised for hot dishes and blanched for salad. Lamb, pork and beef are also important aspects of the cuisine.

Two cheeses, the Coulette d'Avesnes and the Maroilles are famous, and the *andouillette* is a specialty. You'll find a more Northern European attitude here: more worldly, more attuned to cultural variety. Nothing expresses this better than the most famous product of this area, Champagne. This remarkable improvement on what was a rather mediocre white wine produced on the cold chalk hills around Epernay has stunned the world. Almost 200 million bottles are produced each year, many of them selling for more than US$20 (£10) at retail. It's got to be good. The UK alone buys 10% of the production and the USA just slightly less.

The Alsace and Moselle

Northeast of France, territory often disputed with Germany, is home of the *quiche Lorraine*, an egg pie that seems synonymous with French cuisine. But the staple of the region is pickled cabbage (*sauerkraut*), hot potato salad and sausage, real testimony to the Germanic heritage, as is the Alsatian language, a German dialect also spoken on the other side of the Rhine. But there is plenty of French influence in the *pâté en croûte* and *mousselines*, and the Alsatians will tell you they are French, not German.

Pork is also a staple, from which a wider variety of sausages are made than in Germany. There is even a "sweet and sour" style of cooking meat with fruits here, dating back to the 16th century.

Goose is a favorite autumn dish, stuffed with apples or chestnuts. The goose liver is made into a *foie gras* that rivals Perigord's. In fact, this region is considered the source of forced-fed goose liver, credited to the Jewish community here, which needed a substitute for pork fat in their cooking and found it in goose fat. Fresh fish is often prepared cold, *en gelée*.

The wines of the Alsace are white, dictated by the cool summers. Both dry and sweet, they are low in alcohol and are considered by some to be the best whites of France. They are named for the grape rather than the location from which they come: Sylvaner,

Riesling, Gewurtztraminer, Muscat, Pinot... Beer, of course, is the other local drink, a lighter one than those of nearby Germany.

German-named pastries (*kugelhopf, kaffeekrautz, birewecka*), *pain de Gènes, madeleines* and the *macarons de Boulay* are all famous local desserts. The clear *eau-de-vie* made with various fruits, Mirabelle from yellow plums, Kirsch from cherries, serve well as *digestifs* after these heavy meals. Sweet liqueurs, made from the same fruits, are recognizable for their characteristic fruit colors. These are considered medicinally beneficial.

The Münster cheese comes from a specific valley of the Vosges and gets its strength from the character of the local cow's milk. It goes well with Gewurstraminer.

So this region has a Germanic character, lightened and complicated by the French influence. Expect some obstinacy in Strasbourg, but not much. After all, they are dedicated to their cuisine.

The Alps

Another region of France close to a border country, in this case Switzerland and Italy, also takes a part of its character from its neighbors. Hay and cattle are the crops here, Gruyère, Comté and Emmenthal cheeses being the results, and cheese fondue and cheese soufflé the evidence at table.

The staple meat, however, is pork, made into Chamonix ham and a variety of sausages. The fish from the streams are full of bones, so the meat is made into *quenelles*, or fish cakes. Many dishes are served in the gratin style, with milk and cheese. The walnuts of Grenoble are AOC, and a liqueur is made, flavored with their flesh. Chartreuse is also from this region, an herbal liqueur flavored with saffron, cinnamon and mace.

Wines from the northern part, the Arbois, are great with Morels (*morilles*), and the other mushrooms of the mountain forests: *girolles, trompettes de la mort* and *cèpes*. The rich red Rhone wines, to the south, are marvelous with all this cuisine.

Burgundy

South and west of Alsace, at Dijon, the Burgundy wine district begins. Here are the famous red Burgundian and Beaujolais wines, made from pinot noir and gamay Beaujolais grapes, respectively, as well as the white Chablis (made from sauvignon blanc) and the white Burgundian chardonnays. In this century, no other wines of France have had a greater impact in the world, eclipsing even those favorite clarets of Bordeaux. Dijon and Lyon have been gastronomic centers since the 14th century when Dijon became famous for its mustard.

Along with the wines are the tan Charolais beef cows, perfect for *boeuf bourguignon* and indigenous to this area, though now raised all over the world, and the famous chickens of Bresse. Wild fowl, frogs, snails and fresh water fish are also local specialties. The *escargots de Bourgogne* live in the vineyards, feasting on grape leaves all summer and hibernating under the vine roots in winter. They are usually harvested just a few weeks after they begin hibernating, when their systems are clean, but they are still plump.

From Nevers comes the *nougatine*, a lovely dessert. Lyon is a chocolate haven. The sweet *crème de cassis* made from black currants is the local liqueur from which the Kir, a dry Burgundian white wine with a tablespoon of the liqueur, is made. Among cheeses, there are the Bleu de Bresse, Saint-Marcelin and Rigotte de Condrieu all made from cow's milk. Picodon is a goat cheese from Montélimar.

The Auvergne

The center of France receives less travellers than most other regions, being the high mountains of the Massif Central. The cuisine is based on dairy products, pork, potatoes, cabbage and wild berries... real country fare. Good, strong cheeses, uncooked and pressed up in the mountains, abound: Cantal, Salers and Saint-Nectaire. Two blues, Fourme d'Ambert and Bleu d'Auvergne, are also AOC.

The Limousin oak provides cooperage for Cognac, and the Limousin cattle is one of France's famous beef. Pork products and sausages are popular. "Given the climate," says Anne Willan, "the cooks of the Massif Central go for calories rather than finesse..."

People of Auvergne are tight-fisted. They come to Paris, work in dingy cafés and save their money. Certainly they've made a killing with some of their products. The mineral waters of Perrier and Vichy spring from these mountains, around the old spa of Vichy. Badoit and Volvic are also locally produced and all are controlled by their AOC. The Limagne valley is an original source for frogs, whose legs are still fried and eaten here, and known all over France.

Cognac and Bordeaux

Moving across to southwest France, the famous wine regions of Cognac and Bordeaux, is to visit a land uniquely mixed with British characteristics. In the 12th and 13th century, this Aquitaine region was part of England. Since then, when Bordeaux was the fourth largest city in England, it has been a cosmopolitan and prosperous center of trade. Though the Bordeaux wines have been outshouted by the Burgundies, they are still unsurpassed. The great *Grand Cru* vineyards around the city produce some of the most famous wines in France, from the complex, dark reds of St. Emilion, Margaux and Château Mouton-Rothschild to the elegant sweet Sauternes. The crisp white Bordeaux from the Graves and Entre-deux-Mers are equally pleasing.

In cuisine, one returns to the oysters of the sea coast, which are raised at the water's edge, then brought inland to fatten and mature. They take their names from these maturing villages. The Marennes oysters have a green meat. The *entrecôte* of the Bordelaise complements the red wines, as does the St. Emilion chocolate charlotte.

The Chabichou goat cheese is remarkable and the Charente is both dairy country and home of Cognac, the great brandy of France, different from an *eau-de-vie* in that, after distillation from wine, it is aged in wood barrels, instead of crocks, thus taking on a golden color. *Foie gras* and truffles come from this area, as well as elsewhere in France, but the *truffe du Perigord* is considered the best. The Gascogne was home to Cyrano de Bergerac, the archetype of the Frenchman: chivalrous, generous, reckless, brave, irresistible to women, vain and boastful.

The Pyrenees

So far from Paris are the mountains separating southwest France from Spain, you would expect major cultural differences. The Basque people are still demanding independence in their mountainous homeland on the southwest extreme of the Pyrenees, high above Biarritz. They are the originators of the red beret, which is now synonymous, to outsiders, with the French in general, but still very much in evidence in the Basque country, along with a cuisine closer to the Spanish: red peppers, vegetables cooked with garlic and salted fish. Once the Basque people hunted whales in the Bay of Biscayne. Hot blooded people.

At the bottom of the mountains, in Béarne, is the hearty country fare of a *poule-au-pot*. (The famous béarnaise sauce was actually invented in Paris, though named for this region.) And *confit* is another: salted meat or game cooked and preserved in fat.

On the other side of the Adour river is Armagnac, a grape brandy aged in wood barrels, like Cognac, but whose character is slightly sweeter. (In a blind tasting of 12 Cognacs and Armagnacs, I choose the latter, every time.) They even make pastries with it.

The local cheese, *fromage des Pyrénées,* is red-skinned when made from sheep's milk and black-skinned when made from cow's. Both are AOC.

The Languedoc

Originally there were two Frances, split by their languages and indicated by the way they said "yes". The *langue d'oil* to the north used *oui* and those in the south used *oc*. Today the Languedoc includes the Mediterranean coastline, west of the Rhone river, to the Pyrenees. They are most famous for their heavy bean soup, *cassoulet*, and *bourride*, a fish soup rich with garlic and olive oil. The land is so rich here and the sun so plentiful, they can get three crops of vegetables, but the most important crop is winegrapes. The Herault, Roussillon, Corbières and Minervois produce most of the basic red table wine the French love: immature and rough. Perhaps this is an unfair assessment of the people, themselves, however.

In the stark, poor hills above the Tarn, it's sheep country, as it has been for years. Anne Willan reports a *pot-au-feu* called *cabassol* made from lamb's head and feet. Economy is still a primary consideration in much of this area, in contrast to Toulouse, now capital of high technology in France and home of the Concorde. The candied violets of Toulouse are now a popular export item. And in the north, the Ardèche is home of the famous chestnut cream, *marrons glacés*, as well as home of the Roquefort cheese, made in limestone caves with sheep's milk and protected by law since 1411. (For the real thing, look for the little red sheep on the package.)

So what have we here? In the countryside, a simple, strong, direct farm folk and yet in Toulouse, all the sophistication of candied violets. The Languedoc is a fusion of the basics with the best.

The Provence

Home of the great seafood stew *bouillabaisse*, this is a cuisine of strong contrasts: peppery, garlicky main dishes made with olive oil, and balanced with fresh, cool tomatoes (only considered edible since the 19th century), fennel and eggplants. Ratatouille was born here. The herbs of Provence grow everywhere: lavender, rosemary, thyme, sage... and anchovies, olives and capers add to the list of major flavorings. Melons and figs are AOC. There is abundant evidence of Italy here, both in the cuisine and the warm ways of the people.

The lovely rosé of Provence is also AOC, as are the deep reds and flinty whites, though it is the rosé that is my favorite, made from a blend of red grapes brought by the Romans and as old as Persia, which are quickly pressed and the skins removed to give that light salmon color. Light and full of humor, the rosé reminds me best of the Provençal lifestyle, as do Pernod and Ricard. Flavored with anise (licorice), the latter turn cloudy in water, like the outlawed *absinthe* and the Greek *ouzo* and the Arab *arak*.

The southern French people are considered lazy by Parisians, who give little credence to the laid-back ways of the Mediterranean coast. But with such lovely cuisine, who wouldn't spend all day at table? For more on Provence, see the films "Jean de Florette" and "Manon des Sources". Or read "Letters from my Windmill" by Alphonse Daudet.

If we haven't convinced you, by now, of the need to travel around France to get a picture of it, we give up!

WINES AND THEIR PLEASURES
"A meal without wine is like a day without sunshine."

The stereotypical post-war Frenchman starts his day, "killing the worm", with a shot of red wine followed by an *express*, the thick, bitter coffee in the tiny cup. Every bar in France serves this peculiar combination, though it's mostly older, working class men who adhere to the tradition.

Alcohol kills more people in France than road accidents. It is the number three killer after heart disease and cancer. Except for breakfast, however, no French person would consider a meal without wine. One million Frenchmen produce two billion gallons of wine a year, one quarter of the world's total. They consume more wine per capita than any other people on earth. From the time a child is old enough to hold a glass, he is allowed to share in the enjoyment of this beverage at family celebrations, though he must be 14 to be served in a restaurant. Yet over-indulgence is not tolerated in polite company. You will rarely see a French person "drunk", either at home, at a party, or on the street, though alcoholism is indeed a serious problem.

The French have no better tolerance for alcohol than anyone else. They consume a great deal of wine, but nearly always along with food, taking a glass or two at two meals during the day rather than four glasses altogether at cocktail hour.

Wine is not a typical cocktail in France. Before a meal, you'll be offered an *apéritif*, usually a wine-based sweet product like Dubonnet, or vermouth (which is what the French mean when they say Martini). The current favorite is a Kir: a Burgundian mix of white wine sweetened with Cassis, a black currant liqueur. Otherwise, whisky. Many today prefer a *jus d'orange* or Perrier water.

Wine complements French food. The tanin in red wine melts the rich fats of French cuisine and blends deliciously with meats and vegetables. Quality is not usually an issue of pressing importance to the French consumer. Laws established at the time of Napoleon guarantee a certain standard of quality and most people just order the house wine. There are the "wine snobs" who analyze every nuance and can distinguish among the years and vineyards of Burgundy and Bordeaux, but you'll find more of these among the English than the French. In fact, winesellers in France often complain of the lack of discrimination among their countrymen. The people who pay the most for French wine are the English and the Northern Europeans. Consquently, most of the great wines of France are sold outside the country.

Simple red wine is cheaper than beer, by the glass, in France, both in bars and restaurants. It's everyman's beverage.

Wine is such a basic part of life in France, people take it rather casually. A Frenchman will analyze and criticise his meal long before he'll worry over the similar subtleties of the wine served with it. This is a shame, because French wines offer a wide range of characteristics. If you know a bit about them, you will enjoy being able to pick and choose from the wine list.

Learning French Geography in a Glass

The complex world of French wines is a great way to learn the geography of France. Winemaking is a 2,000 year old tradition here, and most French people prefer the wines of their own region. Thus, many of the most interesting wines in France are consumed in their own villages. As you travel around, you will meet these wines and come to love them for their happy association with the people and the countryside from which they come.

If you cannot travel, or you return to Paris hoping for more regional wine adventures, you will find "wine bars" now, each featuring wines from a particular area. In Paris, a handful of wine shops cater to the wine connoisseur, whose understanding and curiosity lead him to specific villages and vintages.

The price of wine goes up along with quality and demand. You pay more as you become choosey about the particular wine you want to drink, especially if your favorite happens to be from the fashionable Burgundy region. There are many good French white wines other than Chablis and Pouilly-Fuissé, but people know these names and order them, and their price is based on demand. The wine bars and your own explorations around France will help you find interesting wines that are not prohibitively expensive.

For the less discriminating consumer, most restaurants offer one or two wines from each of the major regions. They won't be the best from each region, of course, but they will have regional characteristics, thanks to French law. Most visitors (as well as the French) do a bit of wine exploring on a menu, then settle on a few regions they particularly like with particular dishes. For instance, I prefer a Bordeaux with a delicate meat dish like veal, and a Côtes du Rhone with a piece of steak. With hearty country casseroles, I'll opt for a Beaujolais or a Touraine red.

Once you get to know the basic regional wines and learn the difference between a Beaujolais and a Côtes du Rhone, you'll have enough command to read a wine list in any but the most intimidating restaurants.

How Wine Came to France

The Phoenicians first brought wine-making to France, following the Mediterranean coast, colonizing Marseille by 620 BC, then moving inland along the Rhone River. Loving wine and planning to stay, they brought a variety of grape vines with them and planted them along their way. Some of them, like the syrah and the muscat, originated in Persia. All these grapes were vinifera, specifically for making wine. The Romans continued this civilizing tradition, 500 years later.

All the great wines of France are made from vinifera grapes: cabernet sauvignon, chardonnay, sauvignon blanc, merlot, muscat, pinot noir, johannisberg reisling and chenin blanc. Often several types of grapes are blended together, and until recently, the wines that resulted from these blendings were known only by the name of the region in which the grapes were grown and the wine produced. Now, following an American custom, the French are naming some wines by their grape name.

Most wines in France are place-named, and those names carry real meaning. Since Napoleon's time, the regions in which the grapes are grown, the kinds of grapes used, and the grape-growing and wine-making practices, have been more and more strictly defined by law. The tiny vineyards of Bordeaux which produce *Premier Grand Cru* wines sell for a fortune, although their drinkability may be well expired if they are more than a couple of decades old. This is the absurd end of the effort to sort out the good, better and best wines of France. But learning some wines by their place names, and finding ones you particularly like, are part of the fun of being in France.

121

Though wine collection and appreciation has developed a serious snob appeal, especially among the English, there is no reason to be intimidated about wine in France. Except for a tiny fraction of the huge production (those *Grands Vins* of France which are hard to find anyway), French wine is very accessible and strictly a question of your personal curiosity or preference.

Learning about the wines of France should be a light-hearted, haphazard trial-and-error experience, strictly for pleasure. There's no such thing as a "wrong" choice for a wine with a meal. The rule of thumb is white wines with white meats, red wines with red. But you don't have to follow it. You might find a few wines you don't like, but it will be fun finding the ones you do. The French don't take their wines too seriously and neither should you.

How To Choose Your Wine

In any French restaurant, the wine list, which is located at the end of the menu, usually looks like this:

> *Vins Blancs (White Wines)*
>> *Sancerre*
>> *Muscadet*
>> *Pouilly-Fuissé*
>> *Chablis*
>> *Vin de Maison*
>
> *Vins Rosés (Rosé Wines)*
>> *Tavel*
>> *Provence*
>> *Vin de Maison*
>
> *Vins Rouges (Red Wines)*
>> *Bordeaux*
>> *Burgundy*
>> *Beaujolais*

Côtes du Rhone
Aude
Vin de Maison

The *Vin de Maison* in each category is the simplest, the house wine, and usually the least expensive of the selections. It is usually available by the quarter, half or full carafe, a full carafe being a litre container, more than one person can drink in a sitting. Most other wines on the list will be sold by the bottle, though some, especially the reds, may also come by the carafe. An honest restaurant will open the bottle for you at the table, and let you look at the label to be sure it is the one you ordered.

Generally, more robust wines stand up to hearty fare. Lighter or more delicate wines are at their best with more delicately flavored dishes. Yet a complex wine can take either a very complex dish or a very simple one. There is NOTHING wrong with drinking a white or rosé with steak, if that's your preference! Don't be intimidated by those wine snobs, even if your waiter happens to be one.

Telling Wines Apart

Let's start with the whites on our list. The differences between these wines are not great, but you may find you prefer one over another. Pouilly-Fuissé, named for a small village in Burgundy, will be the most expensive, because it has become popular as a French chardonnay among Americans. It is one of hundreds of French wines made from chardonnay grapes, and there are plenty of others to choose from. Chablis, named for a small region southeast of Paris, also specializes in whites, made from chardonnay.

Several excellent wines come from the Loire River valley. Sancerre will be fruity and may be a little spritzy, made from sauvignon blanc, while the Muscadet will be bone dry. The house wine will probably be a blend from the south of France, young but drinkable.

The rosé wines in France, especially those of Provence, are actually the closest to those wines first made by the Romans two thousand years ago. They are usually a blend of different red grapes, and the only reason for the light color is that the skins are removed when the berries are first crushed. Most red grapes have white juice, and to create a red wine, the winemaker leaves the skins in the tank after the grapes are crushed and as they ferment. It is the skins that give the red color.

So, in the Provençal rosé, you'll find some of the character of a red wine, but it will be lighter and perfume-like. The rosé of Tavel, which is a village north of the Provence, in the Côtes du Rhone region, will have a more robust blend of red grapes. The house rosé will be a more simple wine.

Among the reds, you'll find a wider variety of flavors and prices. There is a constant debate between Bordeaux and Burgundy wine lovers about which is best. They are made from different grapes. The Bordeaux wines, known as "Claret" in England, are almost 100% cabernet sauvignon grapes blended with 5% to 20% merlot, a milder flavored red grape. The Burgundy wines are made from 100% pinot noir grapes. Both result, in good years—1978, 1983, 1985—and with proper aging—at least three years—in intense, full-bodied wines.

The best wines of each of these regions have been further specified by their particular village, and even their particular vineyards. The Margaux wines of the Médoc region of Bordeaux, for example, can only be made from a few vineyards around that village west of the city of Bordeaux. Same for a Meursault or a Gevrey-Chambertin from those villages in Burgundy. As a result, each has developed a certain character that some serious students of wine can distinguish, blindfolded. This is where we must leave you to plunge into the complexity and richness of French wines for yourself.

The Beaujolais wines are made just in the southern part of the Burgundy region, but from a very different grape: the gamay Beaujolais. This produces a lighter wine, which is drunk young. The *Beaujolais Nouveau* is the ultimate example of this, a wine drunk within a few weeks of harvest. But that is only sold, and should be consumed, before the following winter is over. Normal Beaujolais wines are good for three years and are quite popular in France.

Côtes du Rhone also produces very popular, more intense red wines. The most famous of these is the Châteauneuf du Pape, and all the wines of this area are made from a blend of up to nine grape varieties. These are usually a good buy in reds, compared to the Burgundies and Bordeaux.

The Aude region is a relatively new grape growing area and has not enjoyed the prestige of an AOC designation, which specifies a vineyard area, its grapes and its grape growing methods, by law.

However, the good hot summers in the Aude produce fruity, sweet grapes and the resultant wines are often very good, especially for the price. They tend to be a little fruitier and more alcoholic than other French reds. And they are usually sold young.

Which comes to my pet-peeve about wines in restaurants, in France and all over the world. Most of them are sold too young, long before they are fully developed. It is a waste of money to buy an expensive Bordeaux or Burgundy wine that is only two or three years old. There are plenty of good, inexpensive red wines to be drunk in France that are at least five years old. To pay more for what is a "better" placename, but then drink a wine that is too young, is not worth it. Often, restaurants do not put the vintage date of their wines on the wine list. Some wines don't have a vintage date, but they are always the cheapest ones. Don't be bashful about asking for the vintage on any bottle of wine, other than the carafe wines, of course. And give a good white wine at least two years and a red at least three or four years to age properly before you drink it.

Some Words to the Wise

Especially when it comes to wine, you can't be sure what is in the carafe. For *pichet* wines, you will quickly learn to tell from the characteristics, whether it is a Côtes du Rhone or not. But when you order a specific bottle of wine, with a specific date, you should always expect the bottle to be uncorked at your table.

— Chapter Seven —

HOME LIFE

FAMILY AND THE LIFE CYCLE IN FRANCE

"In France a man's privacy is sacred—even on the street."
—Luigi Barzini, "The Europeans"

Like all people, the French have a unique way of seeing themselves, within the family construct. Their view is quite different, for example, from the American view, even though from the outside it appears to be the same. Some of the differences have been brilliantly explained by Raymonde Carroll (op.cit.). Here we blend some of her insights with comments and notes from various sources.

The Family

The French put family first. It is a social cement and a specific, personal duty outside of public life and the philosophy of politics, art and cuisine. Although French people can be very romantic about love, the business of marriage and children tends to be approached in a very practical way. The French look to their extended family for emotional and economic support. So the marriage is a building block of that extended family, not something to fulfil one's personal emotional needs.

However, marriage is not the major threshold into adult life; having children is. Children constitute the parents' obligation and link to the society at large, especially in the middle and upper classes. Children also put a burden of obligation on the parents to their respective families.

Children

The obedience of young children, especially in public or in the presence of their parents, is still very important. Their behavior, good or bad, reflects on the duty of the parents to the society. Children must respect their parents' wishes and the father is always right... at least in appearances.

Other people's disapproval of a child reflects directly onto the parent. Children will be reprimanded in public, often to show other adults that they are trying to do the job correctly. In the absence of the parents, other adults will quickly feel invested with parental responsibility. Young French children are carefully watched by the parents. Parents will even go along to music lessons and sit in, monitoring the child's progress.

French parents are not playmates to their children, as in some other cultures. Their job is to civilize the child, who in turn seeks companionship among his siblings and other children. Each member of a French family has a unique relationship to all the others, however, and it is up to each member of the family to act as go-between in misunderstandings. Often, however, one child or parent becomes go-between in all disputes, as the recognized wise and rational one in the group.

Disputes among the children usually must get worked out among themselves, without parental interference. That way, they learn the function of the "go-between" role and they also learn to stick together against authority (the parents, then later, the government).

Then, at adolescence, children are rewarded for their apprenticeship into civilized society with a freedom to experiment and explore. They are still supported by the family, and live at home, but each is allowed his independence. Parents and other adults will still correct the children, even verbally abuse them, but they usually let them go about their business. Since the child's conduct reflects on the parents, they will continue to intervene on behalf of the child through his school years. Even in university, parents will try to participate, and after the children are married, the parents will often help them out with housing or other expenses.

"The French support their children until they are stepping on their beards," says one British friend who has lived in France most of his life.

Confused visitors may find themselves being treated as French adolescents. They may be reprimanded or scolded in public for doing something the wrong way. By giving his personal attention to a stranger, the French person will feel he has shown a parental interest in the erring visitor and satisfied the French sense of adult responsibility. But visitors often mistake public correction as a rude intrusion. Criticism, especially in public, seems out of place to most visitors and, in any case, none of the French person's business.

Stepping Into Adulthood

In France, maturity means parenthood. Young people, married or single, remain in an "adolescent" stage until a first child is born from a sexual alliance. Only then does one move from childhood to

129

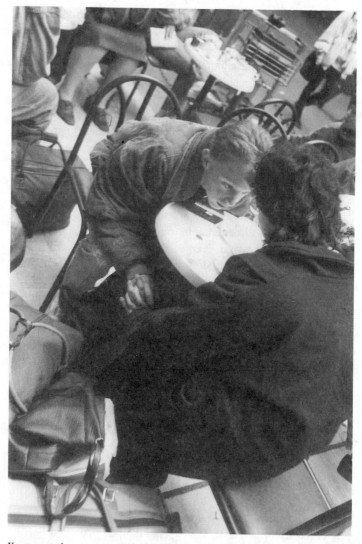

Young people are not considered adults until thay have had a child.

adulthood. Then the cycle begins again, and the newborn is now the younger generation.

This does not imply that sexual "coupling" is not taken seriously. The public pronouncement of a couple, inside or outside marriage, implies a serious change in social category in France. The relationship of couples to their world of friends becomes a part of the private/public dichotomy in France. After establishing the fact, verbally, that they are a couple, the further details of their lives together, everything that makes them a couple, will not be subject to public discussion. Passion and intimacy between them is reserved for the home, or for a totally anonymous situation (as in a couple kissing when walking down the street). Being a couple does not mean they will do everything together, or even walk particularly close to each other. They will reserve the things that make their relationship special for their private time together.

In public, couples act in a normal, individual French way, expressing their opinions, showing their emotions. They will participate in lively discussions. They may either criticise their partner or show particular concern for the other, without reflecting on the status of the marriage. To show the special nature of the solidarity between them, they will make each other the butt of their jokes.

When entertaining with friends, at home or in public, the group situation takes priority. In fact, friends will often "test" their friend's new partner to be sure he (or she) is suitable for their friends. They will also test to be sure the new couple does not try to exclude any previously established friendships. A couple's relationship is equivalent to a friendship or a sibling relationship, with the added element of approved sex.

For that reason, couples who argue, when among their friends, are considered to be acting normally. The French say there is only one step between love and hate. Love is exhibited better by passion than by harmony. One displays indifference to one's enemies. Harmony, which is an important public persona for married couples

131

in many Western cultures, can look like indifference to a French person. It could appear to indicate boredom in the marriage. And the French dislike being bored, as we know.

Old Age

As the parents age, they slowly (and not without protest) switch roles, becoming the responsibility, the children of their children, but never the friends, the equals. That is unusual. Given the way children are raised, friends are sought only among one's peer group. But friendships are a special category we will see in the next section. This parent/child role reversal can come quite early, by other cultures' standards. Many people, when they reach 35, find their parents already calling them for advice and being obedient to their suggestions.

As the French now prefer smaller families, they are also experiencing the "nuclear family" syndrome: older members of the family

Enjoying the parks is a family pastime in France, for locals and visitors alike. Dogs and children are welcome, but don't sit on the grass.

retire and move south, away from children and grandchildren. As they come to need assistance, they move to hospices, rather than burdening their children. But the traditional Sunday lunch, with the whole family gathered together at the grandparents' house, is still a "command performance" wherever it is still possible. If not, a telephone call, at least, is expected. Evidence of this is still clear in the city parks of Paris, which will be nearly empty on a Sunday morning until after the noonday meal. Then, they will flood with families... all generations, strolling together in a group, all dressed up and deep in conversation.

On Sunday morning, the street vendors do good business as households prepare for the traditional family lunch.

BEING A GUEST IN A FRENCH HOME

You've been invited to a French home for dinner. BOY! Are you lucky! Few people, even French people, get such invitations. The French home is traditionally very private, so an invitation for dinner implies a high level of intimacy. Most French people reserve home entertainment for family and very close friends. The size of Paris apartments is one practical limiting factor and the expectations of the cuisine another. The French usually go out to a restaurant with their friends, something you can suggest to your French acquaintances if you would like to establish better contact. Never ask to visit someone's home if you haven't been invited. If you want to stop by, for some reason, telephone first.

Another reason you may not be entertained at home, is that your French friends may feel uncomfortable about trying to cope with someone's manners and expectations different from their own. This is changing, now, with the younger generation, but it still holds true in many social circles, especially among Parisians.

If you are not invited to a French person's home during your stay in France, don't feel offended. Some of the most famous internationals living in Paris, including Gertrude Stein and Henry James, mostly befriended other internationals. A century ago, James complained that though he had been invited to the *salons* of Flaubert and regularly met Zola, Maupassant and the other illuminaries of the day (he was also well-known by then), they always treated him as if he were a stranger, as if he weren't there. He complained to his family, as he finally left Paris to live in London, "It is rather ignoble to stay simply for the restaurants," implying that he was never asked to French homes. But Henry James also said very positive things about his Paris life:

"You know, you get all ready to hate the French—it happens all the time when you live in Paris—then they'll turn around and say something or joke about themselves, and you like them all over again."

Behaving Like a French Guest

Once you are invited to a French home, remember these basic rules. They will help you get invited again, and thus help you establish a friend for life.

1. Arrive at the appointed time. If it's for dinner, you'll probably be invited for around 19:00 or 19:30 hours. In some Parisian circles, later.

2. Dress as you would for going out to a restaurant for dinner; the later the appointed hour, the more fancy the dress code. For the men, a suit and tie are usually sufficient.

3. Don't arrive empty handed. Bring a plant or flowers (in odd-numbered amounts, often seven, but never 13), but not chrysanthemums (which are reserved for funerals), carnations (bad luck) or red roses (reserved for lovers and close friends). Bring good chocolates or a good bottle of French wine. The French quickly recognize quality. If you bring sparkling wine, make sure it is Champagne, or a very good sparkling wine from your own country. It's not "just the thought that counts"; the gift should be something the person wouldn't indulge upon himself, something that appeals to the aesthetics or the intellect, but also nothing embarrassingly extravagant. A present for the children is also a nice thought.

4. Finding the address: Remember that numbers on buildings in Paris increase very slowly. Number 20 may be a long walk from number 2, and often there is a 2bis following a building numbered 2 and before a building numbered 3, all independent addresses. Don't forget to ask for the door code, as most residential buildings in Paris now have front doors that are locked at night. There is either an intercom or a key pad, on which you must punch the code, before the buzzer will sound and the door unlock. If there is no intercom or code pad, press the button, a buzzer will sound indicating that you can now open the door. The individual doorbells in the building will be inside.

5. You will be welcomed into the living room and offered an *apéritif*... or a "cocktail" borrowed from the English. Don't have the bad taste to ask for wine. Red and white wines will be served with the meal. Cocktails will usually be *apéritifs* of one sort or another, or whisky or a Martini (which is vermouth, in France). An "American Martini" is a Dry. Let your hosts serve you and stand to receive your drink when it comes.

6. You will be introduced to the other guests, often members of the family. Expect a group and be prepared to explain how long you have been in Paris, but don't ask people what they do for a living. That's like asking their bank balance in France.

7. There will be something to nibble, crackers or nuts rather than fancy American hors d'oeuvres (which on a restaurant menu means "assorted vegetables"). The meal may well be an hour or more away, but don't fill up. You'll be expected to eat a great deal later. Ironically, the more fancy the dinner, the less volume there will be, but rich dishes are more filling than simple ones.

8. Usually the French people will not show you around their home. They would consider it "showing off", as well as a breach of the private/public split. You've only made it to first base. Stay where you have been settled in the living room. Don't even follow your host or hostess into the kitchen to help. You can offer to help, but take your host's decline literally. You are the guest and it is his pleasure to serve you. The only other room in the house you are likely to see on this visit is the toilet (the WC, not the bathroom, usually two different rooms). Likewise, don't help yourself at the bar (unless instructed to do so), and don't open cabinets or drawers to look more closely at an interesting book or object in the room. Careful respect for privacy has nothing to do with being an international, this is something the French expect from each other.

9. Now that you have been incorporated into the small friendship circle of this French family, you have an important duty. Your

role tonight will be as a participant in the conversation waltz, explained in more detail in the section on "Conversation".

10. At table, you will usually be "placed" by the hostess; so look for name cards or await her command.

11. Silverware is often placed downward. You should start with the pieces on the outside, and work your way inward. The pieces above your plate are for dessert. Or, another set of utensils will be served with dessert and cheese.

12. Wine will be served with the first course. Once everyone is served, the first sip will be a toast, or at least an acknowledgement (*Salut!*) from the host to his guests. Once the meal has begun, you may want to propose a toast to your hosts, to the evening, or to whatever seems of general benefit to all assembled.

13. Try eating with your knife in the right hand and your fork in the left. It's the French way and it is very efficient, especially with cumbersome salad.

14. You may rest both arms on the table, between bites, but not elbows.

15. Break your bread off from the main loaf, don't cut it. Put the uneaten part or parts next to your plate, so they don't get soggy in the sauces. But leave your bones and bits on there, not on the table cloth or the floor.

16. Comments about the food and the wine are always a topic of interesting conversation. In a restaurant, you can be critical; at home, of course, if you can't say anything nice about the food, don't say anything at all!

17. Try to finish the food on your plate. It is a compliment to the hosts, as is a request for "seconds" unless the presentation of that course is obviously highly staged and difficult to repeat. The meals in Paris will be much lighter than those in the country. Ironically, the very place your request for "seconds" will be appreciated most is in the country, where you are least likely to have room for it!

18. If your host does it, you may also soak up your sauces with your bread, using your fork not your fingers. The same applies in informal restaurants.

19. When you have finished a course, put your silverware together across the plate, fork up. Make your comments on the quality of the dish.

20. Courses will correspond to those in a restaurant. A starter (soup, a fish course, or a mixed salad), the main dish (*entrée*), a green salad, cheeses, dessert, fruit. Wines will be served with all courses, except, perhaps, the salad. A champagne will often be served with the sweets.

21. As the cheese board goes around at the end of the meal, cut yourself a share of the cheeses you want, maintaining the wedge shape. Don't take off the point.

22. Peel and slice your fruit with your knife before eating it.

23. An after dinner drink (*digestif*), a sweet liqueur or a dry distilled product like brandy, *eau-de-vie* or *marc,* will be offered. Now is the time to smoke, if you wish. Ask your host's permission, if no one else is smoking, and don't smoke between courses.

Accidents Will Happen

If you should have an accident in your host's home, say you spill something on a rug or break a glass, you will usually be relieved of the responsibility of that damage. This is another sign of your relationship to the hosts. In the US, a guest would consider it his duty to replace or repair any damages he causes, and he would feel guilty about it. In France a host considers it his responsibility to accept liability for his guests. (Another reason, perhaps, why French people are slow to invite people to their homes!) Offer to replace and repair your mistakes, of course, but don't be surprised if you are told that the crystal goblet was "really worthless", and the hosts insist on putting the matter aside. If you do break something valuable, you might consider sending a nice gift later, to express your appreciation for your friends' generosity. But don't press too hard to replace the loss. It might cause offence. But do write a personal thank-you note to your hostess.

Staying with a French Family

You've been invited to stay! How nice! Now you will see how truly warm and generous the French are.

Just a few pointers, though, in addition to those mentioned above for dinner.

Out of respect for the household privacy, don't wander into rooms to which you have not been shown, including the kitchen. Don't help yourself unless instructed to do so, don't even open the fridge or a cupboard. Ask before using the TV, stereo or radio. Keep the doors to bathrooms and toilets closed. Don't try to be "at home". You are not.

Do help whenever possible, however, with clearing the dishes and washing up.

The French are very concerned about disturbing their neighbors. As a guest, try to behave like your hosts and be particularly concerned about making noise, including bathing late at night. Also, in some homes, bathing still requires a complicated preparation of the hot water. Give your hostess plenty of advance notice, when you want to use the bathroom.

If you are a student going to live with a French family, do not assume automatically that you are being accepted as a family member. Remain respectful of the private space in the home outside your own room. Don't let it all hang out unless behind the closed door of your own assigned space. Remain acting "like a guest" in the company of the family and allow your French hosts to develop the increasing levels of intimacy, at their own pace.

Because there is little private space in France, your presence will be a major impact on the family. Try to minimize that impact, wherever possible.

FRIENDS AND NEIGHBORS

Most French people establish friendships slowly, especially by American standards. As we have discussed earlier, this is not because they are unfriendly, but because a friend is a serious commitment, an extension of one's family responsibilities in life. So be patient and don't try to push your intimacy on people. That forces them to take you in or drop you. You'll most likely be dropped.

Here again we refer to the work done by Dr. Carroll in her book, "Cultural Misunderstandings". A friend in France is what you would expect: someone who loves you like a sibling, whom you can trust, whose company you enjoy, who accepts you as you are. Friends help each other, but in France, friends are expected to do more than give support and sympathy. They are expected to help guide, correct and participate in each other's lives.

Anglo-Saxons often find French friends can be suffocating, always talking on the telephone, always discussing their personal lives in detail and always planning events together. Yet they will rarely analyze the relationship between the two of you. They prefer to discuss other things in life, either problems with another family member or politics or art. Often, such discussions will lead to disagreements, but there is no threat here. Once a friendship is established, it need not be treated so delicately, it will be strong enough to weather such storms.

The French do not worry about being overbearing with their friends, they do not count favors or work hard to keep an equilibrium, a balance of the number of dinner parties or gifts one gives the other. They expect their friends to love them as they are, and the activity of reaching out to each other is more important than maintaining an equilibrium.

Raymonde Carroll notes some interesting examples of this. A good friend calls another, saying she is exhausted. The friend immediately offers to come over, take the children, and allow her friend a few hours' relief.

Friendship demands a great deal of one's time in France. Friends can call each other, day or night, for the slightest reason. When friends use the telephone, it becomes an extension of their relationship, another visit, another chance to connect. French people will call each other, right after they get home from a party together, if they think of something they forgot to say, or they have a bit more news. Between friends, a telephone is a line of love. When a friend calls you on the telephone, he will rarely introduce himself, expecting you to recognize his voice—and thereby establish your intimacy: if it wasn't really you, you wouldn't know who he was.

Friends do things together several times a week. They will introduce their circle of friends to each other and attempt to combine the two circles as much as possible.

As you do become friends with a French person, you can expect to be pulled into his close circle, meeting his other friends, and included in their activities. You will then be expected to fulfil some of these emotional obligations and commitments yourself, as the French expect of their true friends. This can feel suffocating to many people from other cultural traditions.

That's why the expansion of the friendship circle is very clearly limited: one has very limited amounts of time and energy, so one has a limited number of people with whom one can be true friends. Counting many people as "friends" and therefore being very popular, is not the French ideal. It is quality rather than quantity.

Compliments

Many French people are stay-at-homes, thus they are very conscious of their surroundings. Commenting on a pretty dress, a new pair of shoes or the like, is a natural thing to do. French people don't usually compliment just to be polite, but because they really have an opinion about the subject.

Your response should reflect your appreciation of that person's interest. Just to say "Thank you" is to imply, "Thank you, yes I

141

agree my dress is terrific." Too pretentious. Instead, reply with something like, "Oh, do you really think so? I'm so glad you like it!" implying you admire and respect their opinion, whether or not you agree.

Making Your Home Among the French

In the "Practical Information", we will discuss the logistics of living in France, but while we are on the subject of French home life, it is important to mention some of the expectations the French will have of you, when you are living among them, and not on the intimate level of "friend". Here are some tips on how to be a good neighbor, as well as how to keep up with Les Duponts.

Your first relationship in a building will probably be with the *gardienne* who is usually a woman paid to live on the ground floor and care for the needs of the tenants. She usually has her family living with her, though her husband may work elsewhere, and she tends to things such as the mail, deliveries of goods, the mainte-nance of the ground floor facilities like garbage bins, gardens and brass polishing. Having a good relationship with the *gardienne* (or *concierge*) makes life infinitely easier in France, and you can usu-ally establish a good relationship by a friendly manner and thoughful remuneration for any special attention you get, as well as Christmas and Easter bonuses, which usually should be 500 FF to 3,000 FF, depending on the number of ways you are using her services.

The *concierge* will also often be a good source for other service people you need: plumbers, electricians, carpenters. She usually knows who is around and who has done good work in the past in the building. She will also be able to recommend good neighborhood shopping and advise on local gossip.

The people she cannot help you with are the neighbors. These relationships are far more delicate, partly because of the attitude towards friendships described above. Because you are living at very close quarters to the other people in the building, and they cannot

SERVICE £500
FRIENDLY £3000
SERVICE

necessarily become friends, you must establish a certain respectful distance from them. This distance involves a polite acknowledgement of their presence, when you meet in the hallway, stairwell or elevator, but a respectful silence beyond that. The coolness allows both of you your privacy.

Certain considerations will be expected of you: you will want to hold the door for anyone coming in behind you (as most people do, even in the *métro* stations in France). You will avoid making any unnecessary noise in the public areas of the building, as well as in your own quarters, if that noise reaches other apartments. Though you are in your own private space, you will be expected to behave in a way that assures everyone else his privacy as well.

Sooner or later, you will begin to make friends among your neighbors. Like all friendships in France, these will take time. Even in the countryside, you will find people hesitant to step forward. Speak French and be patient.

Meanwhile, you will probably experience bouts of loneliness, especially in the middle of Paris. Here are a few suggestions for combatting this problem:

1. Go to the movies. All movie houses discount their prices on Mondays. Read "Pariscope" or "L'Officiel" for the details.
2. Ask your friends to come visit (few will need to be asked twice) and look up friends-of-friends, who are often glad to meet another international with whom they share someone in common.

Chapter Eight

BUSINESS IN FRANCE

MONEY AND BANKING
"*L'argent n'a pas d'odeur.*" (Money has no scent.)

The French have a very ambiguous and uncomfortable relationship with money. They love sex and are not shocked by any form of it, yet they find the subject of money indecent... the opposite of the stereotypical American. Socially, people with "old money" are more respectable than those with "new money"; in fact third generation nouveaux riches are distinguished from more recent nouveaux riches, but the topic of money is usually not discussed casually.

Although French people dislike talking about money, yet the LOTO, a lottery game, is popular among men and women of all ages over 18. Tickets are sold wherever the sign is displayed.

It is not polite to ask someone what he does to make money. A French person does not want to be judged on that basis. As a business person, you will find that no particular status is awarded to you in France based on how much money you have made or your proven ability to make it. In Hong Kong and New York, money means more than almost anything else. In France, it is more likely to be a source of resentment against you. It is much better to come to France penniless, as an author or professor, if you are seeking social acceptance.

We obviously do not suggest avoiding making money in France. If you are here to do business, you will find the French also ready and willing. But it will help to recognize this ambivalence towards money, from the moment you start buying things in shops, to when you negotiate with banks and finally, in the next section, when you begin dealing with the world of office relations.

The New French Franc

The new (since 1979) French franc is part of the European Money System and its relationship to the German mark is a key one in the EEC, but all currencies fluctuate. The franc is used in France, Monaco, the overseas DOM and TOM areas and many former French colonies which are no longer officially associated with France. However, many people still refer to the old *ancien franc*, especially when talking about large amounts. A million old francs is 100,000 new francs.

Opening a Bank Account

Banking is made as discrete as possible in France, to avoid everyone's embarrassment over dealing with it. French banks look more like second-class airline offices, and French banking personnel dress down, some even wearing blue jeans. There are few protected *guichets*, most use an open counter design, allowing you to be as intimate and casual as possible with the person handling your money. The major security effort is at the entrance, where you will usually have to go through two doors, each opening only when the other is closed. If a bank robber comes in, they simply trap him as he leaves, between the doors.

To open an account, you must be 18 years old, have a valid piece of identity (passport or *carte de séjour*) and a proof of residence (telephone bill or EGF bill). Most banks offer both savings accounts and checking accounts. Opening a bank account, as an international, is no longer so difficult. You are allowed to hold money in a French account, as long as you can show it came from outside the country, or that you have a *carte de travail* that allows you to earn French money. Bank transfers between countries are ridiculously slow and expensive. Use traveller's checks or go the electronic route: use your home bank via your home VISA or American Express or Eurocheque card. Ask the French bank to withdraw francs from that card and put the money into your French account. Most card com-

147

panies won't charge you for this service and most banks honor the best rate of the day on the exchange.

You will receive your checks in a few days and your *carte bleue* (CB, the name used in France for a major credit card) in a couple of weeks. Most banks link your CB card to the bank account, so when you pay with your CB, the amount is deducted automatically from your checking account the next month. You can also use the CB card as a cash card at money machines all over France, if you ask for a PIN, or personal identity code number. Some bank accounts, especially at the post office, limit the number of withdrawals you can make in a week, and some machines charge for withdrawals. Some savings accounts, like the *Postépargne*, offer both check writing and cash cards.

Many people in France have their salaries deposited directly into their bank accounts, and their monthly bills, like EGF, telephone, etc, are deducted automatically. Automatic deductions are postponed until you have had ample warning, by mail, that they are going to do so. They are an easy way to get your monthly money chores done.

It is a major *faux pas* and a serious crime to overdraw a checking account in France. Thus, French checks are readily accepted everywhere, often without a piece of identification, making a French account a very convenient thing to have. As the *carte bleue* and other credit and debit cards become more popular, though, these are preferred.

OFFICE AND BUSINESS RELATIONSHIPS
Learning to Work With the French
"As internationalists, we have, indeed, tremendous power, and our home-country business skills alone are no longer sufficient in themselves."

—Robert T. Moran "Cross-Cultural Contact" column in the International Management Magazine, July 1985

Now that we've said a little about the French approach to money, we plunge into a far more complex subject of inter-cultural relations: how you work with the French.

Philip R. Harris and Robert T. Moran's book, "Managing Cultural Differences", is the bible of cross-cultural understanding for Americans doing business abroad. Moran, an American who has lived and worked in France, encourages cultural diversity in business, both to get a better global approach towards the marketplace and to enlarge the pool of management resources. But he admits that working outside one's own culture poses certain disadvantages, including a more complex decision-making process and the risk of poor communications. Much is being written and studied on this subject; see the appendix section on "Culture Shock" and the suggested reading list on this subject.

For now, let's consider the basic problems of working with the French. An international working in another country has suggested five C's of doing business internationally: continuity (a sense of history and tradition), commitment (to the growth of the organization), connections (where social skills and social standing count), compassion (balancing scientific and political issues) and cultural sensitivity (a respect for other ways of doing things). These are the skills which you, as an international doing business in France, should be working towards. Forget capitalism as your first priority, it's cultural sensitivity you need now. The French don't really trust capitalism, just as they don't trust a person based on his professional accomplishments; individuality and personal relations count for much more.

Connections with your company's French branch will put you several steps ahead, when you come to France to do business. The local office can help you with the logistics of work visas, office supplies, as well as local communication and transportation skills. But even with a French office as your helping hand, don't expect to feel "at home" here, in the beginning.

149

Many things, visible and invisible, are different in a French *bureau*: from the paper clips to the filing containers to the standard size of the paper, to the way meetings are conducted. If you are used to the American 8.5 x 11 inch standard of paper, you will find out that the rest of the world uses an A4 standard, which is taller and narrower by nearly an inch. Likewise, the storage of files is handled in boxes rather than filing cabinets. Even computer programs are different.

When a meeting is called, it will be very formally conducted, though the appointed hour may be more flexible than you are used to. Obviously you will have to start doing business, now, in the French language. You may notice that those pleasant French associates, who spoke English so well during your brief visits to France in the past, now take you along for lunch and speak French the whole time. Many of the office staff will turn out to be not as comfortable with English as you had thought originally. From the instant you arrive, your French skills will be challenged. You should start now, gearing up on the French language... as well as on the French way of establishing business relations.

Don't get discouraged when you don't understand everything that is said to you. No matter how good your skills in the language, you may find it difficult to communicate, much less get the job done. The laws of life are invisible and often inaudible in a French office. You must deal with a new game of personal relationships. What motivates a French person? For whom does he feel he is really working? Your affiliation and achievement orientation may be vastly different from his.

Less emphasis is put on individual performance, on the spirit of competition, and on one's identity as a worker. Because most of the French are Roman Catholic, they combine a Latin temperament and Gallic values. Holding several conflicting ideas at once is not unusual for a French person, nor is it considered illogical. Rather, it is proof of a positive sense of flexibility. They may well be indirect in their communication, hesitant to commit themselves to an idea, and yet sometimes very swift to take action. Office organization will be more poly-chronistic rather than linear, a classic distinction made clear by the great cross-culturalist Edward T. Hall. If you have been trained to an Anglo-Saxon or Confucian logic, you will find the French difficult to work with, at first.

Robert Moran compares working internationally with fighting with two swords. At the same time as we use the personality traits that have made us successful at home: aggressiveness and competitiveness, for example, we have to learn to use a second sword of gentleness, cooperation, indirectness and commitment to relationships. The French are not so oriented towards competition; they are innocent of the Puritan work ethic. Yet they are very conscious of job security, social status and being judged as an individual. Time is less linear and the value of time is not measured by money alone.

Thus the very traits that had been your strengths may become weaknesses in France. Harris and Moran describe the rigid structure of French organizations. Authority is more centralized, with individuals having less authority; so decisions are usually reached more slowly. To defend one's position in the system, one may build walls of protection, rather than take aggressive action.

Listening and observing will be your essential skills. Several projects may be going on at once, with the same staff, and only the central authority will be capable of communicating ideas to everyone. You will need to carefully analyze the pattern behind the activities. Your relationship with each member of the team may be a more important concern than controlling organizational decisions. You gain trust and respect through your ability to work with others.

Many international firms here are realizing that profound cultural differences separate their organizations in different countries, even though they may share a common language of business. There are hundreds of different scenarios that will illustrate these differences, in France, but it helps to know a few in advance. Firstly, don't depend on the telephone as a means of serious communication with people you don't know well.

The Telephone As Enemy

Your business relationships in France will probably start on the telephone. This is unfortunate, for though it is the same basic instrument and it functions the same way as in other parts of the world, the telephone in France is not considered trustworthy. The lines work fine. People are just not comfortable speaking across them to strangers, even in French. Raymonde Carroll devotes a whole chapter to this subject in her book, "Cultural Misunderstandings".

When you first call an office or shop, you will often get the impression that you had better hurry up with your questions, that you are taking valuable time away from the person on the other end. They will ask for your name before they volunteer any other information or service, and they may only give a first name to you (thereby remaining anonymous), if you ask for theirs. The telephone pressures the person answering into making a commitment he or she would rather not make.

The French like to put off the moment they must commit themselves as long as possible. A telephone call is similar to having someone knock on your door, unannounced, but worse. At the door, you can use the peephole and see who it is. You can say you were just going out. You can also get an idea of where you stand by watching the person's facial expressions and figuring out what kind of mood he is in. On the telephone, especially with strangers, French people feel very vulnerable and many respond poorly.

Unless, of course, a French person wants to complain. In that case, he will more quickly use the telephone than go in person, as the threatening aspect of the telephone is to his advantage. So, many people use the telephone only when they want to complain.

So, use the telephone to make an appointment, but try to keep most of your business activities on a direct, face-to-face basis.

Company Acquaintances

It is obvious that the French do not depend on popularity in their
business connections. They prefer to pick their friends on the basis
of their personal qualities. Within a company, structured patterns of
authority prevent casual friendship, anyway. (The French are slow
to make friends because friendship implies more commitments and
duties here than in other western countries, as seen in the previous
chapter.) When working in the French company, it is better to be
pleasantly surprised by a co-worker's generosity and warmth. Don't
expect more than he or she can give. That Gallic coolness is a reality
of French life, which is not a popularity contest.

Few office workers will offer the ego-building emotional support you might have enjoyed at the home office. Regardless of your
success and track-record, you will be considered with suspicion at
first, in France. You represent the higher, central authority of the
company, on whom all is blamed and to whom little is credited.
Your secretaries may not be comfortable having lunch with you,
either, as French firms tend to be strongly hierarchical.

Office relations are delicate in France, partly because of the
constant tension of job and class distinction. Although the French
firmly believe in the ideal of equality, the social structure remains
quite rigid.

Always use the *vous* form among business acquaintances and
never use first names, even with your own secretaries, unless the
French person suggests it. If you are unsure whether a woman is
married or not, use *Madame* rather than *Mademoiselle*, as the latter
also implies a spinster. Avoid any but the most polite and patient
approach to fellow workers, and be sure your business letters follow
the formal French code.

That hand-shaking exercise we described in the section on "Non-
verbal Communication" symbolizes the formality of relations in a
French office. The hand-shake implies a small degree of equality
among the French. It is quite minimal in intensity, with little eye

contact and doesn't necessarily imply comraderie. But everybody does it, because some gesture of equality is important.

Security is an essential element of concern to French office staff, more than job advancement or office comraderie. Though he will take his five weeks of paid vacation, he will rarely take a day off without pay. He will stick to his desk, his job and his position.

If you are coming from the home office, you will be treated with a certain esteem. You will then be expected to behave accordingly. Trying to establish equality and comraderie around the office is not going to work. Remember the star pattern of architecture and organization in French life. Your job is to uphold your part of the web of relationships, according to the French expectations. Take each of your relationships at the office as unique and delicate, being careful not to accidently strain the links of communication and function before you can recognize them.

Don't try to impress people with your accomplishments; boasting is condemned in France. Try to direct attention away from yourself towards the specifics of your role in the business at hand.

Watch for subtle signs of class distinction in your co-workers and business acquaintances. The social structure of France is still organized around the peasant, artisan, bourgeois pyramid, with the titled classes at the top. Respect these roles by maintaining yours as an outsider.

Your first goal is working together. Don't let someone's haughtiness bother you. The French play a class distinction game with each other all the time (see the section on "Getting Respect"). Those who feel secure will rarely resort to such masking. You don't need to humble yourself. You just need to be aware of these social masks of life in France in order to work with people effectively.

As you begin to understand office politics better, you will come across a system of connections called the *piston*, which is the way the French describe being pushed forward in one's career by a helpful superior. This is quite popular in France, a way of seeking out the "cream", but not always an equalitarian approach. You will find fresh starters beginning at different levels in the company, depending upon their *piston*.

Business Meetings & Negotiating

Business meetings in France are conducted in a formal way. There is a strong sense of protocol. Proper demeanor is critical. The person who takes charge of the meeting is the central authority. His job is to hear all opinions and to reach some compromise that is deemed fitting to the overall plan.

Though decisions are made from the top, during the course of the meeting, all opinions should be aired. Each person must be careful not to overstate his case, lest he take time away from someone else's opportunity to speak. (Refer back to the section on "Conversation".) Discussions may get far more heated than they would in your business meetings at home. The person chairing the meeting will usually remain passively listening.

The French consider negotiation like a grand debate, Bob Moran says. At the conclusion, well-reasoned solutions are to be found. Yet often after heated debate, nothing spectacular will be concluded. Sometimes, in what seems to be mid-debate, the subject may change completely, leaving the whole issue hanging. Don't worry. Such airing of opinions is an important part of solving a problem. Remember, silence is also sustaining. A great matter will take a great deal of time to consider. It is impolite to insist on one's opinions. It is far more important to reach an appropriate and favorable compromise, at the end. Let's break for lunch.

Having Lunch

"*Ventre affamé n'a pas d'oreille.*" (A hungry stomach has no ears.)

Lunch is a great place to establish good relations with your French associates. Few would consider a meal without wine and this gives everyone an opportunity to relax and get to know each other, putting the office problems aside. Consequently, arriving at an office just before lunch hour will not endear you to the hungry staff, nor will arriving too soon after lunch, when everyone will be a bit lethargic and unwilling to attend to you. Suggest lunch, instead. Your French co-workers will be most interested in where they are going to have lunch and the quality of conversation at lunch. Often the subject of work will not even be discussed. Lunch is a time for enjoying the senses and the intellect, for feeling alive. There is more to life than making money.

Who pays the bill after a business lunch?

Taking each other out for lunch is a common gesture among business acquaintances in France and most French people will not protest your paying, if you state your desire clearly in the beginning. In better restaurants, the waiter will look around the table and decide which person is supposed to pay the bill. That person will get a dollop of wine in his glass before the waiter leaves the bottle on the table. If you are paying and you do not accept a glass of wine, you make things difficult for the waiter!

Drink wine, but remember, inebriation is not acceptable. Even if you don't want to drink, accept the first glass and sip it slowly, or order a bottle of water as well. A bit of wine relaxes everyone.

At table with business associates, avoid questions about people's personal lives, but don't be surprised if they immediately divulge their political views and want to hear yours. Politics is a favorite topic of conversation (see "Conversation") and one guaranteed to raise passions and inspire the intellect... just the ticket for lunchtime entertainment.

Your opinions will be particularly enjoyed if they disagree with everyone else's. Criticism of institutions and ideas makes better conversation material than agreement. The goal is stimulating discussion, a meaningful outlet for tension. Besides questions involving money, avoid personal tales that could be interpreted as boastful or self-centered. Stick to topics allowing everyone to participate.

The French take two hour lunches to talk as much as to eat. The negative side of these great, long lunches is the hours following. It takes two hours for a glass of wine to work its way through your system. So, unless you will be able to take a nap after lunch, don't drink more than a glass or two during the meal. The French who do drink are used to this noontime drinking.

FRENCH LAW IN YOUR LIFE

"Men are born and remain free and equal in rights."

—Jean Jacques Rousseau

157

French law dates from before the Revolution, to the 17th Century reign of Louis XIV whose adviser Jean Baptiste Colbert centralized all power in the palace at Versailles. The Grand Plan of French democracy was described by Rousseau, above, but the Napoleonic Code, the basis of French law today, followed the example of Louis XIV and set his centralized approach into stone. The Napoleonic Code has made for an enormous mountain of bureaucracy, in France, and accustomed the French to filling in endless forms and giving the government information on every detail of their lives.

Whether you are getting a driver's licence or trying to find a job, you will be dealing with the unique and complex legal organization of France. The bureaucracy tries the patience of Job. But be patient, there is method in the madness.

It may be of some consolation that the Grand Plan still exists, the system assumes each man's freedom and equality, although it may take years before it becomes evident to you. The French also complain about the hours of waiting in line and difficulty of getting answers from French bureaucrats. Just take three deep breaths, expect many detours and bring some good reading material along to read while you are waiting. Also be on the outlook for *le système D*. The French take pride in their ability to *débrouiller* the bureaucracy, get around it by resourceful means. This is also known as *contourner la loi*, not following the law. Parking in Paris is a good example.

You will need to come prepared for bureaucracy. Starting at home, be sure to bring with you: your driver's licence, your marriage certificate, your birth certificate, any advanced educational or professional degree certificates you've earned, or your international student ID card, lots of copies of your passport photo, copies of all your bank account and credit card numbers, and copies of receipts of all your major purchases which you are bringing with you, including home computers and other electronics. (See "Home" section to avoid bringing TV's that won't work in France.)

Women's Rights

You will note that the quote at the beginning of this section refers to "men" only. Equality, one of the three principles of French democracy, did not apply to women. The original Napoleonic Code gave few rights to women, and it is only since 1923 that women have had the right to open their own mail and only since World War II that women have had the right to vote.

However, French law protects women in many ways. The Government provides maternity and child care, as well as abortion on demand. After a protest by anti-abortion groups in France, the manufacturers of an abortion pill took their product off the market. The French Government made them put it back on the market, arguing that it was an important medical advance for French women.

A woman alone with children holds all rights and obligations for the family, unless decided differently by the court. Women who have a third child are rewarded with extra home-help allowances. But marriage and courtship are more formal and both marriage and divorce procedures more complex. A woman keeps her maiden name all her life, legally. She votes and pays taxes under that name, but rarely does she use it, socially.

The role of women in the workplace is still more conservative. Though small, entrepreneurial family businesses are a tradition in France, the male head of the family is still the norm, and that authority carries through into the business world. There are growing numbers of exceptions to this rule, and in principle, the French believe in equal rights for women.

Sending A Registered Letter

A registered letter carries more weight than a personal visit. It is binding legal proof and people feel bound to respond. In general, when doing business with any agency or company, it is best to send a registered letter spelling out (in good French) your complaints or requests. For some things, of course, you must go in person.

Legal Logistics

Catherine Kessedjian, a French lawyer, specializes in the legal needs of English-speaking internationals, both individuals and businesses. She has graciously provided the material for the rest of this chapter. As this is a complex area of French law, we recommend you contact her directly for your specific needs:

Catherine Kessedjian
Docteur en Droit, Avocat à la Cour
27, rue des Plantes
75014 Paris
Tel: 45.40.86.27
Fax: 45.40.56.82

Visas and Work Permits

Your original visa, placed in your passport by the French Embassy in your home country, is good for a three month visit. If you plan to immigrate for any period over three months, you must organize things in advance. Your goal will depend on what you want to do while in France. The best way to go about this is to visit France, as a tourist, and consult with a lawyer there to assess the feasibility and administrative procedure for your return. Find a lawyer experienced in both business and immigration law. As the laws relating to foreign residency rights change quickly and often, what we provide now is based on the law that existed on March 31, 1989.

All internationals who do not belong to the EEC or other special countries and who want to reside in France more than three months must first obtain a *visa de long séjour*. That will require two visits to the French Embassy or Consulate responsible for your home town. The first visit is to pick up the forms, the list of documents to be filed and the list of medical doctors accredited by the French Consulate. Then, when all documents are filled in and the medical examination complete, you must go back to the Consulate to file the formal request, with all your justifications in hand.

Here, the waiting period begins, up to three months usually, during which time you must remain in your home country. Once the visa is granted, you may enter French territory and immediately present yourself to the local *Préfecture* to file for a residency permit. The same documents filed to obtain your visa will be needed. Once you've got the visa, as a student, for example, you cannot ask for a residency permit as a *visiteur*.

There are two kinds of residency permits: the *carte de séjour temporaire*, of one year maximum validity; and the *carte de résidence*, which is a ten year permit with full working rights. In a few cases, you can be granted the *carte de résidence* immediately, but usually you will first be granted the *carte de séjour temporaire* under one of the following statuses. For all of these, you will need

161

proof of a clean police record and a medical examination.

Etudiant   To be accepted as a student you must show pre-registration at a university or graduate school, at least 2,000 FF in monthly revenue from whatever source, a prospective place of residence in France, and medical insurance, if you are not eligible for student social security.

Visiteur   You must show a minimum revenue of 6,000 FF, a private medical insurance (preferably French), a place of residence in France, an agreement not to work in France either as a salaried employee or in any profession for which special authorization is required. The *visiteur* permit is not to be confused with the "tourist" visa.

Employee   Your prospective employer must file a contract, written on special forms, and various documents, depending on each case, with the Labor Administration. To be sure this is done properly, a specialized lawyer is highly recommended. One copy of the contract, stamped with the authorization, will be forwarded to you. The employer will have to pay a special one-time tax based on the salary paid the employee.

Trader   Whether working as a sole proprietorship or as the manager of a corporation, if you do not hold a *carte de résidence*, you must get an authorization. To do so, you must provide the bylaws of the prospective corporation, a detailed explanation of the business project you plan, proof of financial feasibility and good experience in the field, and proof that you have never been bankrupt before.

Family member   If you are married to an international already authorized to reside in France, you still must apply, in France, for your own residence authorization. This is done through the *Office des Migrations Internationales* (OMI).

Family member   If you are married to a French citizen, you will be granted a *carte de résidence* with full working rights after one year of marriage. Before then, you have the right to reside and even work in France, if you find an employer.

In general, after three years of residence, if your status has not changed, you may be granted the *carte de résidence*. But this does not apply to students.

Renting Laws and Tenants' Rights

Apart from commercial rental contracts, which are handled in a different way, the basic regulations for housing contracts apply, whether or not you are a French citizen. In some cases, you may sign a one year lease, but the standard length is either three or six years. The tenant must give three months' notice of quitting. The owner, six months.

Commonly, the owner will ask for some guarantees (proof of revenues, a guarantee from a relative, etc...). A two month rental deposit is normal, but more is illegal. Fees and expenses of a real estate agency must be split equally between tenant and owner.

It is very important that a thorough, written appraisal of the apartment or house be done before you sign the lease and before your departure, so that the owner cannot claim damages and keep the deposit. This is called a "contradictory" at which both parties or their representatives are present. You must ask for closing bills from the EDF and the Telephone company and pay them, before leaving, otherwise the owner has the right to hold the deposit until you can prove you have paid all the bills.

You must insure your own belongings as well as the apartment or house against fire, water damage, etc. You are also liable for taxes related to the apartment. A tax of 2.5% of the rent must be paid monthly and a flat *taxe d'habitation* must be paid by the tenant who inhabits the apartment as of January 1 each year. That amount depends on the size and location of the building (See the section "Renting an apartment" in chapter 9 for more details).

Buying Property

Very few restrictions remain for non-French people buying real estate in France, except in certain areas or certain types of property (farm land and protected cultural property are the common examples). Deeds must be prepared by special lawyers called *notaires*, though any lawyer can advise you on real estate law.

Taxes for the registration of the deed and, generally, expenses related to the purchase of the property, are paid by the buyer. Apart from the fees paid to the real estate agent (which are calculated from the sales price), you must expect to pay an extra 10% of the property price if the property is to be used as a habitation and 20% if the property is to be used professionally. This is the estimate of the registration taxes and expenses previously mentioned.

For exchange control purposes, if the money used for the purchase comes from abroad, the *notaire* must stipulate it in the Deed. This allows you to export the proceeds of the sale later.

A value-added tax must be paid on the property, based on the length of time you own it. The longer you own it, the less tax you pay. After 20 years, no value-added tax is due.

ESTABLISHING A BUSINESS IN FRANCE

Your embassy in France, or the French Chamber of Commerce and Industry (CCIF) will be able to help you in establishing a business in France. The CCIF publishes a booklet in English describing the basics of French law regarding businesses here. Ask for "How to start a business in France". It gives you, in a very Anglo-Saxon manner, a step-by-step approach to administrative formalities, but you should certainly consider legal assistance. You have a number of choices for structuring a French company.

Various Company Structures in France

Entreprise individuelle	This is the equivalent of a sole proprietorship in US law, and the owner's personal and business assets are both liable. A spouse may become a partner by registering, as well.
S.A.R.L.	A minimum of 50,000 FF and two to 50 shareholders are required for this kind of company. Shareholders' liability is limited to individual contributions.
E.U.R.L.	Similar to the S.A.R.L., this allows the manager to limit his liability to his individual contribution while maintaining financial control.
S.N.C.	General partnerships require no minimum capital and the partners have the status of traders, but each is jointly and separately liable for debts.
S.A.	This is either a privately-owned or a fully public company, with a minimum of 250,000 FF capital, at least seven shareholders and no maximum. If it is fully public, the rules are more strict.

Subsidiaries, Branches and Agencies

If you want to establish a subsidiary company of one currently existing elsewhere, you also have some choices. The subsidiaries are autonomous legal entities, economically dependent on the parent company. Their managers must obtain a *carte de commerçant étranger* or a *carte de résidence* depending on their nationality. In some cases, they must also file a declaration of investment with the Treasury Department before registering. Your company can also set up an agency or branch in France, for whose debts the company is totally liable. For this, you must register with the Trade Register, provide two certified copies of the company's Memorandum and

Articles of Association translated into French, provide the name of the manager of the French branch as well as the birth certificate and French registration of all personnel.

A liaison office is even more informal and registration is not required, as long as you are only establishing contacts, handling publicity and collecting information in France.

Commercial Licences and Employee Requirements

If you are not French and plan to operate as a sole trade, a partner of an S.N.C., a manager of an S.N.C., S.A.R.L. or French branch, subsidiary or liaison office, or the general manager or chairman of the board of an S.A., then you need either a resident's card, an EEC passport or a commercial licence.

If you do not hold an EEC passport, your ability to work in France is strictly controlled. If you are assigned by your company to work in France, or you are coming to France to work for a French concern, you must get a visa before you arrive from the nearest French consulate or embassy.

For individuals seeking to live or work in France, it is essential to get good legal advice, before you arrive. Refer to the previous section on "Law in Business and Life" for more details.

Chapter Nine

PRACTICAL INFORMATION

HOURS, HOLIDAYS & SEASONS
Hours

Inspite of a nine-to-five working day, France still takes *le déjeuner*, the midday meal, quite seriously. Most shops close during the middle of the day for an hour or two. Only restaurants, the post office and the bank are sure to be open between 12 noon and 3 pm in Paris. In the countryside, only restaurants will be open at this time of the day. The French are accustomed to the 24-hour clock, so that would be 12:00 to 15:00 hours. This in no way implies that the French don't work hard. You can find people still at the office until 20:00 or 21:00 in the evening. Many Parisians eat dinner at 22:00 and accept telephone calls until midnight!

Shops often won't open in the afternoon until 16:00 hours, but they will stay open until 19:00 or 20:00. Offices usually reopen after lunch by 14:00 or 14:30 and stay open until 18:00. Save yourself a good deal of frustration by enjoying a nice, long midday meal along with everyone else. Plan to do your shopping errands in the morning or late afternoon.

The post offices are an exception. They open from 08:00 to 19:00, Monday through Friday, and Saturday until 12:00. Banks, too, are open from 09:00 to 16:30, Monday through Friday, though they may close their "exchange" windows at lunchtime. The stock exchange (Bourse) trades from 11:30 to 14:30.

Emergency, after-hours services include:
- Post office: Open 24 hours at 52, rue du Louvre, *1er*. Tel: 42.33.71.60. *Métro*: Louvre.
- Currency exchange: Open every day, 06:30 to 23:00, at Gare de Lyon.

Sunday is Family Day

Sundays are a holiday for nearly everyone in France, except the food sellers on Sunday morning. This is the big market day, as Sunday midday, it is still popular to organize a big family meal. Consequently, there will be no one about town or in the parks on a Sunday until about 14:00 hours. Everyone is going to church, buying food for the meal, preparing the meal or getting dressed and driving to Granny's house for the meal.

The Monday Holiday

Restaurants and other shops open on Saturday or Sunday usually close on Mondays. Don't panic, at least one *boulanger* or *pâtissier* in each neighborhood will open both Sunday mornings and Mondays so the French and other croissant and *baguette* addicts can have fresh goods every day. But you will be surprised to find many shops closed on Monday.

The Year's Holidays and Seasons

Like most Europeans, the French write their dates numerically, starting with the day, then month, then year. The official summer holiday in France starts on Bastille Day, July 14, and goes through the end of August. Paris, itself, moves out of town for the month of August, and you can expect Paris to be deserted that month, except for the tourists and a few restaurants. Some people like this calmer vacation version of Paris. There won't be Opera and other major cultural events, though Mayor Chirac of Paris puts on special events during the summer to try and compensate, but there won't be any traffic jams, either. Expect the seaside resorts and country campgrounds to be packed to the gills.

Conversely, in October, Paris is jammed again with all sorts of special events and conferences. It is often the nicest time of year in France, in terms of weather (it rains more in Paris than in London), but it is one of the busiest, so hotels will be fully booked.

On the major holidays, banks and post offices will close and the long weekend will lure many families out to the highway. Fatalities rise so sharply during these periods, the government has tried to spread out the school holidays more evenly, scheduling six weeks of school followed by two weeks' holiday. However, official holidays should still be noted:

- January 1st
- *Mardi Gras* (Tuesday before Ash Wednesday)
- Good Friday (Friday before Easter)
- Easter Monday
- May 1st (Labor Day)
- May 8 (End of WWII)
- Ascension Day (5 weeks after Easter)
- Whit Monday (8 weeks after Easter)

169

- July 14 (Bastille Day)
- August 15 (Assumption Day)
- November 1 (All Saints Day)
- November 11 (Armistice Day)
- December 25 (Christmas)

TRAFFIC & TRANSPORTATION
Taxis

Paris traffic is the first thing most people experience in France. It is exhilarating… or terrifying, depending on your attachment to this existence. The French appear to have little concern for life or property, once behind the wheel of an automobile, and it is a tribute to their highly developed driving skills (of which they are most proud) that more tourists and locals are not killed.

Not that you should relax. Inspite of these skills, the French kill twice as many of each other per-driver as the British, Americans and Japanese. Such butchery occurs primarily on the major *autoroutes*, but do be careful on Paris streets, even inside the pedestrian (zebra) crossings with the light in your favor. Motorbikes are probable disaster; mopeds rarely obey the rules.

Your first ride will probably be in a Paris taxi… that should be sufficient lesson. Like other French drivers, these men and women, strapped into their beautiful new Mercedes and Peugeots, can stop on a dime, roar to 100 km/h in seconds, and judge their distance to less than a centimeter, just for the thrill of it. They call every one of these techniques into use, as they manoeuver through the Paris traffic. Consider yourself on a carnival ride and be grateful it is that other poor devil out there, not you, trying to cross the street. You'll be out there with him, soon enough.

Taxis are expensive in Paris. The charges add up quickly. Electronic meters calculate the basic price, based on time and mileage, but there are surcharges for any bags put in the boot or trunk, for waiting, and for service on weekends and in the evening. The tip is not included, but the driver will expect 10%. If you are an *ingénu* in France, he may try to shame you into giving more.

Hailing a taxi in busy Paris traffic can be exasperating. It's easier to find the nearest taxi stand and wait your turn for the next one in line. These stands are well marked and taxis are supposed to use them, though a potential customer waiting someplace where it is easy to stop will tempt the driver. At lunch time, taxi drivers also stop for lunch.

Walking...

When you begin walking around Paris (the very best way to enjoy it), keep those first taxi performances in mind. Yes, pedestrians have the right of way, but then there is also a pet poop-scoop law in France, and you will see how effective that is. Keep to the pedestrian crossing and go only when the little pedestrian light is green, at least until you learn the driving dance of Paris traffic.

Driving... The Rules and The Dance

At intersections of equally important streets, not otherwise controlled by stop signs or signals, the vehicle on the right has right of way in France. This is particularly important to know at blind intersections and in roundabouts.

A new rule in France, at major traffic circles like the Arc de Triomphe, changes that right of way. The new rule gives the vehicles already moving around the circle priority over those coming in. There will be traffic lights in front of the entering lane, to control this, but watch for the occasional driver who forgets.

Many traffic signals are delayed in Paris. When the light turns red in one direction, the green light in the other direction has a two second delay. This gives French drivers excellent reason to run through the red. It also gives them good reason to jump ahead of the green. Even with the light in your favor, look carefully before you leap out.

The most interesting part of driving in Paris involves inter-driver communications. Making eye contact with another driver gives the

171

second driver some unwritten right to the road. The person who wants to move into your lane or cross the intersection in front of you, simply avoids eye contact, pretending he doesn't see you, so your rights don't exist. In turn, if you look at him to express disbelief or anger, you acknowledge that you've seen him, thereby giving him the right to go ahead first. This is not a written law, but it might as well be.

Some people say the French treat their cars the way they treat women. Though I am grateful that hasn't been my experience, I must admit I enjoy French traffic, both as a spectator and a participant. From the relative safety of a Paris sidewalk café, one can watch the confrontations, contortions and brilliant near misses with amusement. It is a performance. In fact, café life entertains not just with people, but with traffic, as well.

For some real whopper traffic jams, be sure to be on hand between 7:00 – 9:00 and 16:30 – 19:00 hours weekdays. Friday afternoons on long weekends are particularly outrageous.

What You and Your Automobile Will Need in France

If you do not have an EEC passport, your native driver's licence together with an International Driver's Licence, which you can get through your local automobile association, will be sufficient for the first year in France. After that, you must pass the French driving tests and get a French licence.

Driving laws in France limit alcohol content in the blood to 0.8 (the USA law is 1.0) and penalties are severe, with a current minimum fine of 2,500 FF. Speed limits are: 130 km/h (80 mph) on toll roads, 110 km/h (68 mph) on motorways, 90 km/h (56 mph) on most other roads and 60 km/h (37 mph) in built-up areas. Speeding penalties are a minimum 1,300 FF fine, and the police can do things like stamping your toll card with the time you pass one booth and see what time you arrive at the next one.

Your car must be registered in the town or *arrondissement* where you live, again by going to the *Préfecture de Police* with your title (*carte grise*). To get French licence plates, take your registration to any garage and they will make up plates for you.

Every year in November, you need to buy a new tax sticker (*vignette*) to put in the inside lower corner of your car's front window. They can be purchased from any *Tabac*. You will also need the insurance sticker in that same corner, and copies of the *Constat Amiable* carried with you, in case of an accident. Unless someone is injured in the accident, you and the other driver simply fill out one of these forms, accurately depicting what has happened, sign it, and send a copy to your insurance company within 24 hours. If someone is injured, dial "17" on any telephone for help.

If you have registered your car in another country, you have six months to get the car re-registered, but you must carry proof of registration and international insurance coverage, anyway.

Parking in Paris

Most of the streets of Paris are marked into blocks with the word *Payant* written in them. Rarely will you see one of these blocks without a car sitting in it. Sometimes you'll see two cars squeezed in. If you are so lucky as to see one empty, quickly drop your car in there and look for the nearby box from which you extract your parking permission. You will need 10, 5 and 2 FF pieces, and put in the amount you need for the time you intend to stay. The box then ejects your permission slip, with the time stamped on it, and you place that on the dashboard of your car, visible from the sidewalk. There are also underground parking facilities, marked with a big "P" which operate in a similar way.

There aren't enough places where to park a car in Paris, even though most cars on French streets are quite small. So people have taken to improvisation. In fact the Parisians take up the parking problem with imagination and creativity. They make a game of it. The more clever the breach of the parking law, the better the status points for the driver.

One summer evening, I was dining outside at a narrow, five-street intersection in Paris. Two of the five streets came together at a sharp angle, forming a triangle of extra pavement before the streets actually merged. Several small cars were wedged illegally into that space, and the city fathers had dispatched a tow truck, that particular evening, to clear them off.

We restaurant clients sat captivated for hours as this tow-truck team performed their duties, removing one vehicle at a time. Yet the number of parked vehicles never diminished.

A Paris tow-truck is a remarkable machine, forked, with straps that are placed around the chassis of a car that allow it to pluck a vehicle from the most inaccessible space. We watched the performance over and over again, as each time the truck left with one car, another would shortly arrive and innocently take the bare place. The driver would then strut away with a grin of accomplishment on his face, and we would smile slyly and wait for the truck to return. None of us ever considered warning those poor devils as they sauntered off. It just didn't seem *kosher*.

It was very good drama, a modern Myth of Sisyphus, performed through the night and into eternity, no doubt by a faithful team of civil servants. It certainly inspired me to stick to my perferred mode of private transportation in Paris, the bicycle.

Cycling

From the pedestrian's perspective, a cyclist in Paris is a lunatic. But cycling in Paris, at least for an experienced city cyclist, is much like cycling in the countryside of France: it gives you a wonderful relationship to your environment, allowing you both speed and intimacy.

Everybody is nice to a cyclist in France, even the fast-dancing drivers of Paris. I used to credit this to their passionate love of the sport of bicycle racing. But now I've learned there is actually a law giving two-wheeled vehicles favor over four-wheeled vehicles in a court of law. So, if an automobile hits a bicycle in France, the driver is likely to have to pay the damages.

Whatever the reason, Paris traffic is manageable to an alert urban cyclist. Drivers respect (or endure) your presence, and you have several advantages. You can slip between the lanes when traffic is clogged, speed along on major boulevards when traffic is moving, and even use the bus lanes, which are off limits to everyone excepts buses and taxis. I have found I can usually arrive sooner than both *métro* and bus riders on my bicycle, and I have an advantage, late at night, of always having transportation home. For bicycle purchases in Paris, there is a good bike shop run by English-speakers: *La Maison du Vélo*, near the Gare du Nord. Tel: 42.81.24.72. For bicycle rentals in Paris:

Paris Vélo
2 rue de Fer Moulin
75005 Paris
M: Censier
Tel: 43.37.59.22

The countryside of France is nothing short of magnificent on a bicycle, and there are easy ways to get you and your bicycle into the countryside from any train station in Paris. The S.N.C.F. allows you to take your bicycle along on any ticket. Most *banlieue* trains have hooks in the ceiling from which to hang a bicycle. Beyond the suburbs, there is a small handling charge at the baggage department. The S.N.C.F. also rents bicycles at most major stations around France.

Public Transportation: Buses, Métro *and Trains*

The French philosophy of *égalité* really shines, when it comes to moving people around on public transportation. Even in Paris, service is excellent and everybody uses the *métro* and the buses. For that reason, Paris addresses usually note the nearest *métro* stop as part of their address. Also, people are generally polite in the *métro*, holding the doors for those behind them, allowing those leaving the train to get off before they get on, and giving up a seat for an elderly person.

175

Some buses offer an outdoor back deck, perfect for sight-seeing and picture-taking, or just enjoying the sunshine.

Except for pickpockets, even in these crazy times, the *métro* is quite safe and very easy to use. There are *Métro* and *Autobus* stations everywhere and the maps are easy to figure out. Find the place you want to go to and write down the name of the last stop made on the line that will take you there. Jump on the train or bus with that name and number. If you have to use more than one line, look for the intersection of the lines, that's your *correspondance* and there, find your second line. Both the numbers and the name of the last stop made going in each direction always identify the bus or train you need. To get out, look for the exit marked *Sortie* and orient yourself by the excellent maps at the ticket level showing the exit locations at each station.

The first day you come to live in Paris you'll want to buy a *carte orange*. This gives you unlimited access to Paris underground stations and buses for a month. The *carte jaune*, on the other hand, is a weekly commuter pass, 12 *aller/retour* trips. Which one is cheaper for you really depends on how active you are. Bring along a passport photograph and go to any *métro* station. Children under 10 pay half price. If you want to splurge, buy a first class week's tourist pass, which will allow you in the less-crowded middle car of each train during weekdays, from 9:00 to 17:00 hours. Other days and times, those cars are accessible to everyone.

For just intermittent trips, buy a *carnet* of 10 yellow tickets in the *métro*. Single tickets are available on the bus, but they are twice the price. These must be passed through the gate or punched on the bus when you use them (*composter*), and long bus rides require one ticket every two sections, which are marked on the route map on the bus.

Buses are boarded in front and exited in the middle. Many buses stop at 20:00 hours, and all buses and *métro* services stop by 1:00 and don't start again before 5:30 hours. Service hours are noted at each bus stop. During this time, of course, taxi fares are at their highest rate (23:00 to 6:00 hours).

Likewise, trains in France are clean, fast and inexpensive. The TGV (*Trains à Grande Vitesse*) go at a speed of 300 km/h and zip from Paris (Gare de Lyon) to Marseille in four hours. They are twice as fast as a car and half the cost of a plane journey, and service is constantly expanding, making yet another star pattern of services in and out of Paris. Don't get on board without a reserved ticket!

Suburban and conventional trains leave from all six different Paris stations, each indicating their direction outward. These stations are enormous places, filled with people rushing to catch trains, so watch out for pickpockets here, too, especially as you stop to admire the architecture. The only other nuisance about public transportation is the *grèves*; halting work to protest some labor dispute is common practice in France.

PICKPOCKETS & LOST & FOUND

There are pickpockets in the *métro*, and elsewhere in Paris. They are especially active during rush hours (7:00 – 9:00 and 16:30 – 19:00

177

hours). Keep your valuables out of reach, avoid crowds if possible and be alert for tricks to distract your attention (dropping change, asking for the time, etc) which allow another guy to go for your wallet.

If you do lose something, there is a central "Lost & Found" in every town, including one for all of Paris:

Service des Objets Trouvés
36 rue des Morillons
75015 Paris
M: Convention.
Open Monday – Friday, 8:30 – 17:00 hours.

Go in person to make your claim, between two days and a week of your loss. Expect to pay a charge, based on the value of what you have lost, and a 10% tip to the finder. For your own protection, keep records of the numbers of your credit cards and identification of items of value.

PUBLIC COMMUNICATION SERVICES
"It's the little things in life that drive you crazy."
—American poet Charles Bukowski

The Post Office – La Poste (PTT)
Nothing frustrates foreigners as consistently as the French postal system, partly because we are all used to the way our home postal services work, and the French system is quite unique. Suddenly a little detail of life like a stamp takes on enormous proportions and that sunny yellow sign over the post office entrance, those yellow postal boxes and yellow postal trucks become symbols of torture.

The French postal system actually works remarkably well, considering the round-about way in which everything seems to be organized. Most remarkable are the hours: open from 08:00 to 19:00 hours Monday through Friday and 08:00 to 12:00 hours on Saturday.

But now to that organization. Remember the star pattern discussed in the section on "Arts & the French Psyche"? French postal services are organized in a star pattern, each service is a point on the star, all leading to the center, somewhere in the back room.

When you walk into the post office, your first question will be: "Which window do I use?" If you pick the wrong one (the wrong point in the star), you will wait in line for your turn, only to be told (usually with little sympathy), that you are at the wrong *guichet*, and you must go to the back of the line at another (usually indicated by number), where the services you want are provided. Essentially, you started down the wrong street.

If you need more than one kind of service at *La Poste*, you will usually need to wait in more than one line. However, these different windows will become more familiar to you in time, and eventually, a trip to the post office will only take fifteen minutes, instead of a long, frustrating morning.

Here are the usual choices and services:

- *Poste Aérienne*. This window will take your letters and postcards, weigh them and apply the proper postage, using a very ugly machine-generated piece of tape. Each 5 grams makes a difference in the cost, so you'll have to get your postcards and letters weighed to find out what value of stamps you need. You can ask for a *tarif* which gives all the charges. At each post office there is a scale outside the service windows, so you can weigh your own letters and figure out the cost.
- Letters within Europe and the UK go airmail at *tarifs speciaux* (surface mail is *ordinaire*). All letters can be registered (*recommandé*), insured (*valeurs declarées*) or sent COD (*objets contre remboursement*). You just need to stand at the right window. Letters within Paris are usually delivered the next day, and a day later within France.
- *Timbres de Collection*. This is the window for buying regular stick-on stamps as well as the pretty, commemorative stamps that the PTT is continually producing. Ask for *beaux timbres* and give the franc denominations you need. They also have aerogrammes,

179

overseas folding letters with postage printed on them, and pre-stamped domestic postcards (*cartes postales pré-affranchies*) at this window, but you will have to buy other letter-writing supplies at a stationery store. They do not weigh letters at this window. (You can also buy regular stamps at any bar, press center or *brasserie* where you see the *Tabac* sign.)

- *Paquets*. For mailing small parcels, magazines (*journaux*), books and brochures (*livres*) or other printed matter (*imprimés*), you need this window. The PTT also sells very strong and substantial yellow packing boxes in various sizes for a nominal sum. They are usually on display, with prices attached and you can buy them from this window or the *Timbres de Collection* window. You must then step out of line, wrap your parcel and wait in line, again, this time at the *Paquets* window, to mail it. You'll need to fill out the little green international contents sticker for customs (*la déclaration de douane*). Ask for it when you buy the box, and be sure to describe the contents, as prices vary based on what is inside. Books and magazines, for example, get a cheaper rate. You can also insure the contents (*assuré*) at this window. Make your packages light, less than two kilos for small packages, less than five kilos for books and printed matter.
- *Postexpress* and *Chronopost*. These are the French speedy delivery services, competing with things like DHL and UPS, domestically and internationally. You can send up to 25 kilos with a COD value up to 4,000 FF and *Chronopost* gets packages to New York the next day, after noon. *Postexpress* gets packages up to five kilos anywhere in France in 24 hours, and they will pick up from your home or office (*Allo Postexpress*). Get details at these windows.
- *Postéclair*. This is the new fax transmission service offered by the PTT. Unfortunately, the person you send to cannot reply back to you by the same way.
- *Poste Restante*. This is the general delivery service, for people without home addresses or in need of postal boxes. Here is also the

"will call" window, known as *Retrait des lettres et paquets.* If you get a notice in your mail that a package is waiting for you at this post office, bring your notice, your ID and wait at this window.

- *Caisse d'Epargne. La Poste* in France functions as a bank, as well. You can open an account, get a *Carte Bleue* credit card and withdraw money via the cash card machines outside many of the post offices. Inside, you can get money orders (*mandat international*) in various currencies, wire money, and some post offices will change money. You can also pay your telephone and EGF bills here. (See "Money and Banking" section for more on how to get a bank account.)

- *Téléphone.* For many years, the post office served as most people's only long distance telephone facilities. Many people still use the telephone service at the post office, especially visiting foreigners. The charge is the same as what you would pay for home service (there is a surcharge in bars and hotels). Wait at this window, explain where you are calling, then you will be assigned a telephone booth (by number). You then go to that booth and dial your number. France has only one area code, and that is for Paris. If you are in Paris, you must dial the prefix "16" for calls inside France but outside of Paris. If you are outside of Paris calling a number outside of Paris, just dial the eight digit number. To call Paris from outside Paris, dial "1" and the eight digit number. Dial "19" first, for all calls going outside of France. Rates go down after 22:00 hours in France. You pay at the end of your call, waiting again in the same line.

The simpler, new way of calling inside and outside of France is to buy a *Télécarte* at the same window. This is a credit card with a designated value that can be inserted into the new public telephones all around France. Just insert the card, face up, close the window, and when the digital display of the telephone shows the amount of units on your card, dial your number. The value is reduced automatically, as you talk, and the units of time remaining appear on the digital display. You can also buy a *Télécarte* at some *Tabac* shops, banks and department stores. Look for the *Télécarte* sign on display.

Having a phone card means you don't need exact change, and you don't risk getting cut off, when you run out (if your card runs out of value, just insert another one). You can also take advantage of evening discounted rates. You'll find many of the coin-operated telephones in France, especially in Paris, have been vandalized. Often only the card-operated ones are working. The important thing to remember is: don't leave your card in the slot when you hang up!

IMPORTANT telephone numbers:

• Police and ambulance: 17
• Fire: 18
• Operator: 13
• Reverse charge calls: 10
• Telegrams: 14

ENGLISH LANGUAGE telephone services in Paris:

• Telegrams: 42.33.21.11
• Restaurant reservations: 45.77.63.63

Private Telephone Services
The Minitel

The telephone system of France is a wonder. Not only is regular telephone service reasonably priced and remarkably convenient, but the French also offer an "online" computer system, available to every telephone subscriber, called the *Minitel*. You'll see them in every French office and many French homes, these little computer monitor and keyboard sets. They even have one for your use at the post office.

Their most useful function for the newcomer is as an on-line telephone directory. You can look up any telephone number in France by dialing "11" and turning on the *Minitel* monitor, then tapping the name and city of the person you want onto the *Minitel* screen. The cost of this directory service is based on the amount of time you are "on line". The first three minutes are free.

You can also book trains and hotels by *Minitel*, but it's a bit trickier and you'll need to understand more French. There are *Minitels* in many hotels, now, as well as in post offices, and there are loads of other services available, from checking your stocks to checking the weather, from shopping for food to soliciting sex.

Installing Telephone Service

Although the PTT is also the telephone company, you don't go to the post office to order a telephone. You go to the office in your neighborhood called *Services Commerciaux des Télécommunications*. These are listed in the yellow pages telephone directory at the post office and they are usually very nice offices, again organized in a star pattern, but in this case, you start at an information (*Accueil*) desk, explaining what you need and giving your name. Then you sit down in a nice plush chair there and wait to be called. (Take a book or newspaper.)

You must show formal identification plus proof of residence, either an EGF bill in your name, or letters written to you at that address, or your rental agreement. You then have to know: what kind of plugs are installed already in your apartment, how many telephones you want and what style, whether you want to be listed in the *annuaire* (which gets you on the *Minitel* automatically), whether you want a *Minitel*, and where you want your bill sent and how you want to pay. If you pay by automatic deduction from your bank account (*prélève-ment*) you need to bring proof of your bank account (*rélevé d'identité bancaire*) as well (there's usually one or two in the back of your checkbook). Installation usually takes a few days.

NECESSITIES OF CLEANING UP
Toilets—The Public Ones

France is one country where this subject deserves a whole chapter. Until recently, French public toilets were notoriously smelly old tin structures, where men (and men, only) could take one step off the

The new vandal-proof public Toilettes *offer clean and convenient facilities. The door opens when two francs are put in the slot. Step in, the door closes, lights and music come on. Push the button inside for the door to open again.*

sidewalk, pee, and continue down the street, often zipping up as they went along. These *pissoirs* were basically a hole into the underground sewer system, with a bit of water dribbling along with. No longer!

A rising sense of hygiene and the issue of women's rights resulted in the sparkling new *Toilettes* you'll see everywhere in France, now. A modern white plastic tube, these facilities are a tribute to French ingenuity: they are spotlessly clean and nearly vandal-proof.

Insert two French francs in the slot, and the handless door slides open, receding into the curve of the structure. Step inside the seamless, all white, brightly-lit cavity, and the door automatically closes. Music plays. The toilet-like seat is used in the normal manner, but there is no flushing to do. Push the button to open the door, and once you've stepped out, the door will close again and the entire room will be flushed and cleaned chemically, ready for the next user.

The French have gone from the ridiculous to the sublime, as far as public toilets go. These new *toilettes* have got to be the cleanest public facilities on the planet, including Japan.

However, not all the toilet facilities in France match this standard. In fact, there are plenty of smelly old W.C.'s around. For some reason, the French adopted the English term "Water Closet" or W.C., and some facilities are just that: a closet with a hole in the middle of the floor and two foot pedestals on either side: "Turkish toilets" in English. Though the deep squat position they require is said to be anatomically preferred, they take a bit of getting used to.

You will also have to use your ingenuity as to flushing arrangements. A pull chain from a reservoir over your head, a push button on the reservoir behind the bowl, a pull lever on compressed tanks, a button to step on in the floor... all these variations exist in France.

Partly because of years in the old *pissoirs*, French men can be rather casual about privacy during such activities. In many older restaurants and cafés, men and women must share a common toilet. A urinal may well be next to the hand-washing bowl, convenient for the men, but a bit awkward for the women. In most cases, now, there will be a door marked for *Dames* or *Femmes* and one for *Messieurs* or *Hommes*. Most have toilet paper, but do carry tissues.

Another common difficulty is the lighting system in public toilets. Because electricity used to be very expensive in France, many energy-saving techniques were developed. A common one is in lighting the usually windowless W.C. The light comes on automatically when the door is closed and locked, and goes off when the door in unlocked. You must risk locking yourself into a pitch dark room, of course, but if you haven't found a light switch, shutting the door and throwing the lock will probably do it.

Many café and restaurant *patrons* frown on your using their facilities, however humble they may be, unless you are a paying customer. At least buy a coffee for the privilege.

Toilets in trains are usually passable. In fancier places, or places where there is a good deal of public traffic, an attendant may be positioned at the entrance to the toilets and demand a franc for their use. In such cases, you can expect cleaner facilities and toilet paper provided.

The Private Ones

Private toilets also come in various shapes and sizes, often in a room separate from the bathroom. Be sure to ask for the *toilettes* not the *salle de bains*. Your hotel room will cost quite a bit more, if both private bath and toilet are included.

In hotels and private homes, you will find another curious fixture, a French invention known as the *bidet* (Pron: bee DHAY). This looks a bit like a toilet and, like a toilet, is designed to be sat upon, but is for cleaning oneself, nothing else. A spray of warm water (you must adjust the temperature, so sit facing the faucets) shoots up from the middle of it, and in the days when weekly or monthly bathing was the norm, the *bidet* must have been the ultimate in personal hygiene.

Now that so many of us take daily showers, the *bidet* is a bit redundant, but people who like them, swear by them. In older hotels in France, you will get a sink and a *bidet* in your room, but neither a toilet nor a bath. You'll find those somewhere down the hall.

It is very bad form to use the *bidet* for anything other than cleaning oneself or one's clothes (by filling it up like a laundry sink). In fact, even doing laundry by hand is often discouraged. Laundry dripping on the floor might leak through to the room below.

Laundry Services

Laundry service in hotels is expensive in France. You will probably soon learn about French self-laundry services. These are efficient and inexpensive and often combine with dry-cleaning services, which can be done while you are waiting for the washing machine to cycle!

To operate the machines, you usually have to buy *jetons* from the machine with the laundry price on it. One *jeton* is needed for each machine, and they usually can cope with about seven kilos of laundry. Laundry soap is also available at most self-service places, but you might want to bring bleach and softeners. Bring lots of change, as each machine requires its own coins.

After the washing machine is finished, use the *super-essorage* machine to give a minute's hard spin to your wet clothes. This saves drying time, on the next step. Dryers in France are very hot, so watch woollens, nylons, nylon zippers and Velcro carefully. Heavy things like jeans will take two or three coins, even with the *super-essorage*. Plan about an hour and a half, minimum, for a trip to the laundry.

In general, the French sense of hygiene is up to international standards, now. Visitors to France used to learn quickly why the French are famous for their perfumes.

HEALTH CARE AND SOCIAL SERVICES IN FRANCE

There are three main branches of government services, as they relate to you and your family: health care, retirement and unemployment pensions and family allowances. Employers, employees and the state all contribute to pay for these services and even if you are not a French citizen, you have rights to any of them, for whose services you and you employer are paying.

There are both public and private health care services available. You pay directly for treatment and medicines, then you are reimbursed by the government, if you are eligible. If you are not, you should not come to live in France without some kind of health insurance, preferably one that includes repatriation coverage for returning you to your home country for extended care. You won't get a visa to live in France without your own health insurance.

The American Hospital in Paris is an English-speaking hospital in Neuilly. It is much more expensive than French hospitals, but is acceptable to most American medical insurance policies. The Hertford British Hospital in Lavallois-Perret specializes in maternity cases and its staff are bi-lingual in English and French.

The Women's Institute for Continuing Education (WICE) at the American College in Paris has a very complete book, "Health Care Resources in Paris", which is worth buying if you are going to be in France for any length of time. Copies are available at WICE.

French hospitals have a fairly relaxed pace. Doctors give patients ample stays and patients are expected to supply their own pajamas, robes, towels and toiletries... even for their babies being born! Medicine is freely administered and the price of both medical supplies and services are government controlled.

Medicines are sold through the *Pharmacies* displaying the green cross. The people working in these shops have medical training to advise you on common medical problems. They can even provide you with prescribed medicines, based on your complaints. But if they think you should see a doctor, they can also recommend appropriate specialists in the neighborhood, both private and public. They are also responsible for explaining how to use your doctor's prescriptions, and can even advise you on whether or not the mushrooms you just found in the woods are edible!

Emergency medical care is *Service d'Aide Médicale d'Urgence* (S.A.M.U.) and the Paris number is 45.67.50.50. If your case is not life-threatening, but you are too sick to go to a doctor, there are on-call physicians who will come to your home 24 hours a day, 365 days a year, for a reasonable price. For *S.O.S. Médecins* in Paris, call 47.07.77.77.

RENTING AN APARTMENT
What to Consider
Your first job here may well be finding a place to live. Outside of Paris, it is not so difficult. But pressure for Paris apartments is intense. Rents are high and space is quite small. A standard *deux-pièces* is

189

normal for a couple... that's two rooms, not two bedrooms. Kitchens and bathrooms are cramped and modern conveniences such as washing machines, dishwashers and microwaves are considered extras.

Rather than struggling with the general population of Paris in your hunt for an apartment, referring to the newspapers and classified weeklies, you might connect with the American or the British Church here. They have billboards for subletting apartments, buying furniture from other internationals who are leaving, as well as staff and other church members who might be able to help. Word of mouth is often your best bet.

Renting an apartment in Paris can include problems of nightmarish proportions. Rents are high in Paris; not quite like New York, Tokyo and Hong Kong, but close. The biggest problem is finding a place at all.

As an international, your best bet is finding some other international leaving town or going away for several months. Contact the addresses at the back of this book. If you must go out on the street, looking for apartments, here are some things to consider:

1. Neighborhood. The range of characteristics is large in Paris, including some pretty dangerous ones up in the northeast corner (the 19th, 20th and 11th *arrondisements*) where drugs are a real problem. But even in these sections there are very nice places. Rather than hunt all over town, try to find a couple of neighborhoods you like, walk through them to spot *A louer* signs in windows or look for the street names in advertisements in weekly advertising sheets like *Particulier à Particulier*.

2. *Quel étage ?* The higher up the apartment, the more light and air will it receive. If there is an elevator in the building, the flats high up will be expensive. If not, they will get cheaper as you go up. In older buildings, the most elegant apartments are on the lower floors. They will have high ceilings, long windows and interior details. Don't be put off by something on the 5th floor without an elevator, unless you have serious medical problems. You really do

get used to the stairs, and you'll need the extra exercise to compensate for the rich French diet.

3. Noise. Paris streets are noisy. And the main roads through tiny little villages have trucks (lorries) thundering through all night. Consider your tolerance. Most French apartments have window shutters that close out noise, but they also close out light and air. Apartments opening onto courtyards, away from the street, are usually more expensive because they are more quiet, but they may be noisy if there are many apartments facing the courtyard and lots of people using the courtyard as an access. Noise ricochets up those high stone walls.

4. Mail services and *concierges*. If possible, get into a building with the old-style French *concierge* (who will probably be Portuguese, but that doesn't matter). These women guard against nuisances like overflowing garbage, mail delivery and special notices, servicemen arriving, and they will even hold an extra set of keys to your place, in case you lose yours. They are a marvelous breed, keeping you up with gossip, with politics and with protocol, really invaluable to the newcomer. If your building hasn't got a *concierge*, your mailbox will be lined up inside the doorway. Make sure yours locks. Often they are not big enough for magazines and your subscriptions will be left in a common trough. Mail tampering is a problem in Paris, so ask for a locking mailbox big enough for all your mail.

5. Charges. You will have to pay two months' rent in advance, usually, as well as a fee to the agent. Make sure you get all the papers stating what you've paid and what you are due back at the end. See the section on "French Law in Your Life" for your legal rights as a tenant in France.

6. Red tape. France is built on a mountain of bureaucracy. It works, and some of it actually is very sensible. But speed is not the primary consideration. Be patient. Finding an apartment and renting it take time.

MANAGING YOUR HOME IN FRANCE

Partners and children of people coming to France to live and do business have a peculiar set of problems which are different from the person in the family whose job brings him or her here. Having a specific assignment in one's own field of endeavor gives a person a connection to the new culture that often bridges the deepest troughs of culture shock. Unemployed spouses and children, who must go about all of their normal activities in totally new ways, often have many more culture adjustments to make.

One out of three people sent abroad comes home early from the assignment. Robert Kohls says that studies show four out of five early returns from work abroad are because the spouse, not the employee, couldn't adjust. One woman in Paris for six months explained some of her problems thus:

"My husband's company said we could bring whatever we wanted, so I brought everything, right down to soap and toilet paper. Although he said it was silly, that such things would be available here in France, I knew it might be difficult to find the things I wanted. For example, I forgot shampoo and spent two hours and $20 finding what I hope is equivalent to what we use at home. My husband was furious. As a wife here, the very things which I did at home with expertise are suddenly a whole new ball game. I have to reinvent the wheel. None of my expertise in shopping and keeping house in America applies here."

Other wives speak of trying to get comfortable:

"Why didn't anyone tell us it was going to be so hard?" complains one spouse. "I came to Paris expecting a wonderful, romantic experience, and I feel lost and alone. It's much harder to find work, to find apartments, than I expected. My husband has no sympathy with my problems. I feel like an innocent victim, and it makes me angry."

Indeed, women do not have the same status here as in other countries. Gabrielle Varro is an international living in Paris for 25 years. She is the author of a book about international women married to French men. "The Transplanted Woman" examines a number of the problems of intercultural marriages and multi-cultural children. She says that knowledge of the Napoleonic Code is essential for understanding the status of men and women in France. Although new laws regarding marriage and the rights of women came into effect in the 1970s, cultures change at a slower pace. Women can expect to be treated differently in France, both legally and culturally.

Children, too, experience difficulties adjusting to a new culture. They can feel equally isolated. They have left their friends behind and must start in a new school using a new language. Usually, though, children find it much easier than adults. They imitate the new culture more readily, as they are still in the complex process of learning to imitate their own.

Logistics Around the House

Inspite of a large number of nuclear power stations, French electricity is still relatively expensive and considered something akin to liquid gold by the value-conscious French. Be sure to turn off lights and unplug fixtures, whenever possible, in hotels, private homes, and when at home yourself.

In most hallways in private buildings, the French have already worried about this for you. Lights will be on timers activated by the button marked *Lumière*. You push it and lights come on. After a couple of minutes they cut themselves off. You'll be left in the dark. At that point, you just have to find the nearest button to push (newer ones glow). If you are going up stairs, there is usually a *Lumière* button on every level.

France is unusual in Europe, in that the French have both 110 and 220 – 250 voltage systems. The standard now is 220v, but in some older buildings you can still find 110v. The plugs look the same, so ask before you plug in anything.

If you are coming from the USA where 110v is the norm, then each of your appliances will need a step-down transformer between it and the French 220 – 250v wall socket.

When buying *transformateurs*, ask the man at the hardware (*Quincaillerie*) store rather than a hotel clerk or *concierge* who may not understand electricity. A 220v appliance plugged into 110v won't hurt anything, it just won't work. But a 110v appliance will burn out, if plugged into a 220v socket.

The higher wattage transformer you buy, the more appliances you can run off of it. Just add up the wattages of the things you are bringing from home.

The French plug is a round two-prong device, similar to the old German one. The wiring code is brown for live and blue for neutral. Light bulbs (*ampoules électriques*) are either screw-in or bayonet. The French use both.

But there are other conversions that will not be so easy. Television reception in France is the SECAM system, so your television will be useless if you come from a country using the PAL system. French television quality is one of the best in the world (much better than the American system, for example), so you will enjoy having a French TV. Video players must be those that can adapt to several TV reception systems, as well.

Likewise, many of the English language radio programs available in France are on the long wave frequency, which is different from the AM/FM frequencies common in the USA. There are AM and FM stations here, but you might leave your radio behind and buy one when you get here with the long wave option.

CHILDREN AND THEIR EDUCATION

Children are naturally more adaptable and open-minded than adults, but when you put them into a strange, new setting, they are going to look to you as a model for their adjustment attitudes. A positive approach to your new life in France, and doing adventurous new things together, as a family, will greatly help your children, especially in the beginning, before they have established their own new support system.

Clinical psychologist Paul Marcille, who works with family adjustment problems in Paris, says that children will mirror their parents' attitude. Pushing kids out to adapt to their new surroundings won't work, unless you are doing it yourself.

Also, Marcille says, children's needs will vary depending on their developmental stage in life. A very young child will be more concerned about losing his favorite TV programs, than his friends in daycare. An adolescent, who is normally trying to establish his independence from parents and family, will miss his peer group and will probably need your support more than he is able to admit. Your support and sensitivity can affect your child's adjustment skills now, and later on in life. Children rarely have negative reactions to a new environment unless their parents teach it to them by their own example. It has been proven that children who learn multi-cultural skills early in life have a distinct advantage as adults in international settings. One bright young international we interviewed discussed the differences she found between the pretence of friendship she found at the English-language school and the honest, but cooler reception from classmates at the *bilingue* school.

Children below the age of nine pick up new languages as easily as their first one. Most international families who come to France quickly bow to their children's superior ability to communicate in French, even if the whole family started at the same skills level. Recognize the potential problems early, and seek professional help if you don't feel you can handle them. For helpful sources, including Dr. Marcille, please refer to the contacts listed at the back of the book.

Education in France
As a resident paying French taxes, you can take advantage of the French educational system. If you have very young children, you are in luck! The French government offers *école maternelle* for children from the age of two until five, when they enter kindergarten for a year, then the first grade. Although these schools stop for lunch and close

on Wednesdays, there are *cantines* and *garderies* to fill in the gaps for working mothers.

Once a child reaches the age of nine, he starts to learn languages more slowly. If you have such school-age children who do not have French language skills when they come, you might consider an English-speaking school for the first year, moving on to a bi-lingual school after that.

There are a number of French bi-lingual schools (called *bilingues*) which you can consider as an alternative to expensive, private English-language education in France. These *bilingues* get high ratings among international students I've talked to.

If your children are younger than nine or have strong French skills already and if you plan to stay in France until their education is complete, you should then consider a regular French school. The Association of American Wives of Europeans has published an excellent book, "Guide to Education", explaining the whole subject of education in France, available from the American Church or AAWE.

In their booklet, they ask several important questions you should consider when choosing a bi-lingual school:
- What subjects are taught in English?
- Are English classes separated by ability or just age?
- What are the students' record for further education?
- What percentage of students are multi-cultural?

L'Ecole Primaire et Secondaire

Education in France is free at the primary and secondary level and compulsory until the age of 16. The majority (85%) of schools are publicly run. Private schools, most of them run by the Catholic Church, are partly subsidized. The least subsidized private schools are the most expensive to the students.

All schools have a curriculum imposed by the Ministry of Education, but all schools are also different, depending on the student mix and philosophy. The French outlook on education is aimed towards the examination process. Extra-curricular activities are given less consideration.

* *Collèges* are state schools for ages 11 to 15. At that point, higher education is determined by examination.
* *Lycées* teach an academic three year course in higher education leading to the *baccalauréat* examination, which is the pre-requisite for university. Or, they teach a two-year vocational training program.

There is an international baccalaureate, as well, equivalent to the French *baccalauréat*, British "A" and "O" levels and the American SAT.

There are 76 universities in France, 13 in Paris. Two-, three- and four-year programs are available. The three-year program is equivalent to the BA. *Les grandes écoles* are the most prestigious higher education institutions and most senior civil servants and engineers come from them, though there are *instituts universitaires de technologie* offering programs for careers in industry.

Chapter Ten

APPENDICES

CULTURE SHOCK

"*La culture, c'est l'environnement tangible et intangible édifié par l'homme.*" (Culture is the tangible and intangible environment man creates.)

—H. Triandis

Coping with another culture is stressful, and cultural adaptation is a sometimes-painful reality of a multi-cultural life. For international companies, assigning home office personnel abroad is an expensive and complex proposition. Franck Gauthey et. al. say that when such assignees return early, unable to adapt to their new environment, they cost their company between US$25,000 and US$125,000 in wasted capital, not to mention the hard feelings left with clients they were unable to deal with successfully. Yet multi-national companies need leaders who are internationally adept.

Although books such as ours cannot solve the problems of cultural transition, we can at least help you anticipate them and explain some of the reasons behind basic cultural differences, increasing your ability to avoid some cultural misunderstandings and gain cultural awareness and accommodation.

We want to lessen the shock, accelerate the transition, and deepen your appreciation of France. People vary enormously in their ability to adapt to a new environment. Your success will depend, in part, on your previous experience, your education and your innate flexibility as an individual. Some people who find adjusting most difficult actually do a better job of it! They suffer more, perhaps, but they search more earnestly for solutions to the problems, too. With cultural adjustment, if it seems easy, you are probably not doing it right.

In learning to cope with another culture, you will quickly recognize how deep and subconscious your own cultural behavior is, how much what you "are" is actually cultural, not individual. What makes one way of doing things "correct" and another "incorrect" usually depends on cultural learning so deep it is hard for the person inside his own culture to recognize it, much less to explain it to anyone else.

It is a rude awakening, indeed, for the individualistic westerner to realize how much of the unique "personality" and world-view "values" he thinks he possesses are dependent upon the cultural impressions made upon him, subconsciously, before school age.

Whether it is enjoying food, dressing, expressing pleasure, evaluating priorities, each of us naturally acts in ways that conform to our own culture. When we move into another culture, suddenly we have to renegotiate things we have always taken for granted. The basis of all cultural adaptation is getting rid of one's cultural preconceptions.

Take table manners for example. The tools we use, how we use them, what we do with our arms, elbows, hands and mouths, all come as second-nature. So it is a shock to suddenly enter another culture where the habits are different. Many habits must now stop and new ways be observed and copied, just to assume the basic requirement of "good table manners".

Ironically, cultures that are just a little bit different are sometimes more difficult to adjust to. They take closer observation and a strong suspension of one's own cultural values. You might not notice, for example, that the French eat salad with their fork in their left hand, but pasta with their fork in their right hand. However, your French colleagues will notice when you do it another way at a business lunch with important clients. Likewise, the high volume of your voice at table could be a painful and awkward experience for your French colleagues, though nobody would even notice it in New York.

It is always easier for young people to adapt to a new culture (and lose their first one) than it is for adults. Fortunately, we don't lose all our conforming abilities as we grow older, but those abilities definitely decrease. If we are not expecting to have to use them, we are headed for serious trouble.

Adapting to a new culture is much like learning a new language: it takes daily practice and intellectual effort. There are many rewards. By responding positively to the challenge of cultural adaptation, by observing carefully your new surroundings and accepting the job of learning a new way of doing things, your life in France will be enormously enriched.

Life is a series of re-adjustments. Living outside your own culture can expand your perspective on the world. By trying to get comfortable in other cultures, trying to learn other ways of doing everything, you learn much more about "yourself". That is what makes an international life so rewarding and so addictive. Cultural adaptation is a challenge. Like physical fitness, being mentally alert and culturally sensitive is a kind of exercise. The more you practise, the better you get, and the more you understand and fit into other cultures, the broader your universe.

What Is Culture Shock?

Culture shock is only one part of cultural transition. Culture shock was described by P. Bock in 1970 as "primarily an emotional reaction that follows from not being able to understand, control and predict another's behavior".

Dr. Kalervo Oberg, an anthropologist who defined the term "culture shock" in 1960, says culture shock is brought on by "the anxiety that results from losing familiar signs and symbols of social intercourse".

Considered among the founding fathers in the field of cross-cultural communication, Oberg defined several aspects of culture shock for the United States Agency for International Development. To briefly summarize Oberg's findings, there are at least six aspects of culture shock:

1. Strain due to the effort required to make necessary psychological adaptations.
2. A sense of loss and feelings of deprivation with regard to friends, status, profession and possessions.
3. Being rejected by and/or rejecting members of the new culture.
4. Confusion in role, role expectation, values, feelings and self-identity.
5. Surprise, anxiety and even disgust and indignation after becoming aware of cultural differences.
6. Feelings of impotence due to not being able to cope with the new environment.

The Stages of Culture Shock

The pseudo-medical model of cross-cultural stress was developed first by Oberg and others and is still used today. Oberg's model is combined with the U-curve approach, developed about the same time, and described in detail in the book by Adrian Furnham and Stephen Bochner, "Culture Shock: Pyschological reactions to unfamiliar environments".

In the curve, the visitor starts with elation about the new culture, drops down into a trough of depression and confusion, then comes back up with a sense of satisfaction and optimism. This curve can happen many times, in varying intensity and over a varying period of time, but the cycle itself is now considered a normal reaction, though both mental and physical illness may be apparent. Using this model, we create a typical six-month cycle of attitudinal, emotional and physical reponses you may have to France, or to any other country which you visit for an extended period of time.

Pre-Departure
"I'm so excited! Paris, here I come."

Activities	Planning, packing, partying and parting.
Attitudes	Anticipation of new and interesting things. Lessening interest in current responsibilities.
Emotions	Enthusiasm and excitement, mixed with concern for leaving friends, relatives and a familiar environment. Children are particularly apprehensive and uncomfortable.
Physical response	Adults and children running on nervous energy. Difficulty sleeping.

The First Month
"Isn't it wonderful? Even more beautiful than the pictures."

Activities	Welcoming and introductions. New foods, sights, sounds and people. Start learning the language, realizing it's necessary.
Attitudes	Curiosity about the culture and the opportunities. Downplaying the negative comments of expatriates, the inability of waiters to understand you.

Emotions	Euphoria. You are really in France and it is really so beautiful.
Physical response	Some problems with all the food and wine, the condition known as *crise de foie*, a kind of hangover effect from too much rich butter, cream and fat in the diet. Some difficulty sleeping in a new place, with new night noises.

The Second Month

"This post office eats my letters."

Activities	Moving into a permanent residence. Full job responsibilities and settling into a routine.
Attitudes	The charm of the tiny apartment and the exquisite menus of local restaurants start to look different. Growing awareness of what is not available, or what is ridiculously expensive. Impatience with "rude" waiters and "indifferent" shopkeepers.
Emotions	Nervous, uncertain about how to function. Some withdrawal from the French, and seeking the familiar in friends and food.
Physical response	Colds and the flu (especially in winter). Gaining weight.

The Third Month

"I like France but I don't like the French."

Activities	Language skills hit a plateau and seem to stop improving. People still don't understand you and work keeps you too busy to study, anyway. Work performance declines.
Attitudes	Discouraged, irritable, hypercritical. Negative cultural value judgements predominate. Conversations turn into long strings of complaints, stereotypical truisms seem confirmed.

| Emotions | Depressed, discouraged and suspicious of strangers. Very lonely. Culture shock in extreme. |
| Physical response | Extreme fatigue, often illness. |

The Fourth and Fifth Month

"You know, this is actually a very efficient way of doing it!"

Activities	Small victories in work and language study. Ways of getting things done are sorted out. Moments of competency bring hope. (If this does not begin to happen during this time, the visitor will usually give up.)
Attitudes	Constructive and positive in outlook and potential. Accommodation to the French ways of doing things begins.
Emotions	Renewed interest in France and the French.
Physical response	Health restored.

The Sixth Month

"Your first visit? Well, don't miss..."

Activities	Routine established and visits now planned into other parts of the country with visiting friends. Local friendships established.
Attitudes	Maintain basic constructive attitude despite good days and bad days. Plateau reached.
Emotions	The ups and downs of life now accepted as normal, and a growing interest in helping others and reaching out to those who are struggling.
Physical response	Normal.

Many aspects of individual personality and experience profoundly affect this basic formula. Your "cycle" may be quite different, but few people will be able to learn much about their new culture without experiencing troughs of negative feelings and discouragement. Cultural stress can have profound negative effects on people, but it need not be treated as a disease.

S. Bochner has developed a culture-learning model to deal with culture shock that looks for solutions by learning cultural character-istics that apply. Appropriate cultural skills are survival skills, in a way. Without them the international attracts attention to himself as an outsider. Proper awareness, preparation and attitude can help the international accumulate these skills.

HOW TO DEVELOP CULTURAL AWARENESS
Furnham and Bochner describe several training techniques for devel-oping social skills, and thus minimizing culture shock:
1. Information-giving. This book is all about that, and there are more sources in the Bibliography.
2. Cultural Sensitization. Real adaptation comes from observation, but there are ways you can fine-tune your observational skills. The first step is recognizing that invisible difference between you and another person: cultural perspective. Ann Williams-Gascon and Solange Jochum have developed a workbook, "The Cultural Sen-sitizer", for groups and individuals seeking to improve their skills in this area. The Bloom Program, a course offered each October by the American Church in Paris, integrates cultural sensitization with basics on dealing with Paris. Details are available from:
   Ann Williams-Gascon
   Domaine de Sagnes
   07000 Privas, FRANCE
   Paris telephone: 48.28.03.21
3. Understanding the reasons behind actions or attributes of another culture. One of my chief inspirations in researching this book was a new book by French anthropologist, Raymonde Carroll, called "Cultural Misunderstanding". Her wisdom is scattered through-out this book, but here I'd like to quote her five steps for develop-ing cultural understanding:

    a) Clear the deck. Avoid all attempts at discovering the deep-seated reasons for the cultural specificity of such-and-such a group. Although psychology, geography, history, religion and economics may be part of what people "really are", these do not deal with the culture. Just seek to understand the culture, the system of communication.

    b) Be on the lookout. Listen to your own discourse, making judgements about people. "The French are..." No. "I find the French to be like this or that..." Yes. What is true is: another culture does not have the same characteristics as yours. Try to avoid judging these differences as good or bad.

    c) Recognize a "cultural test" which is a sense of strangeness and unpleasantness, opacity in a certain situation. And remember the situation in as much detail as possible, before judgement has given it a broad stoke. Listen and watch with complete attention.

    d) Then analyze the experience to find an interpretation that can be verified elsewhere in the culture.

    e) Finally see, from this analysis, how other aspects of the culture might apply.

4. Learn informally from "old-hands" on site. Always everyone's richest resource. It's informal and some information is better than others, but it always helps to discuss.

5. Formal Social Skills Training aimed at cross-cultural competence. This you will find in the next section on "Training in Cultural Awareness".

Is It Really Possible to Be Multi-Cultural?

Yes! More and more work is being done in the field of multi-cultural life: marriages, children, work and retirement are more and more multi-cultural. There is a common comparison between learning a culture and learning a language, with as many stages of "fluency" along the way. Like being multi-lingual, there are many levels of multi-cultural expertise, but it is a specific expertise and practice makes it easier. People can speak and act in more ways than one. The classic example is a group of Chinese travellers who queue up at a London airport to board their plane, in the British way, but who then scramble wildly for the exit at Hong Kong, in the Chinese style.

An international in Paris

The pitfall to multi-cultural understanding is assuming that cultural differences don't matter. The mediums of TV and cinema are changing dress codes, language, and are even manipulating values, but real cultural attitudes are taught at birth. They change very slowly. Even though the French realize that their culture is no longer superior and their language no longer the international one of diplomacy, they are far from "assimilated" into anything one could define as "European" culture. Businesses gearing up for 1997 are becoming painfully aware of this.

One's ability to fly around the planet quickly and cheaply does not lessen the cultural differences into which one debarks. It takes time and effort to become culturally functional, and years to become multicultural. But in learning to appreciate the cultural essences, you develop the tools to participate in a culture, and in time you can learn to feel "at home" there.

When I finish this book, I leave my pied-à-terre in France for a weekend with my mother in the home of my childhood on the East Coast of America. Then I fly to my own home in San Francisco. From there I continue on to Japan where I have a magazine story assignment. In Tokyo, I stay with my Japanese "family", who have hosted me dozens of times in the past. Finally, just two weeks after leaving Paris, I land in Hong Kong, where I will spend the summer writing about Asia from a small island "home" I return to each year.

In each stop I will be dealing with different friends, different cultures and different jobs. In each I must be able to function and communicate, both professionally and socially. I must rely on previously learned skills, because the flight schedule allows me no time to learn. With my bag of appropriate cultural habits and the support of friends and acquaintances I have established in each of these places, I think I can avoid embarrassing cultural and professional errors.

Cultural adaptation is something like riding a bicycle: once you learn cultural techniques, they become subsconscious, second nature. To the extent that I can function well as an international, I am multicultural. I am not multi-lingual, except at the most primitive level, but I am at a comfortable level of multi-cultural skills. This allows me to make short visits with ease, and longer visits give me the chance to learn more. Unlike riding a bicycle, there's always plenty of room for improving and refining inter-cultural skills!

Between jet-lag and the strain of cultural adaptation, I expect to be a wreck when I reach Hong Kong. But I can enjoy such a whirlwind tour, confident that I can get the work done, because of the cultural skills I have learned along the way

You can do it, too. Furnham and Bochner say that the most effective approach to cultural transition is the one that is the most specific in detail and example. Although our series can only try to scratch the surface of the problem, we can at least give you a starting point. After that, it's really up to you. The general rule is: the more closely you observe and study another culture, the more you will learn. Learn the language, the communication patterns, the family values, the belief systems, the politics, the history. Everything will help enormously. And the payback is your ever-increasing appreciation of France and the French.

Professional Help in Cultural Transitions

In addition to the many aspects of cultural awareness and methods of coping with cultural transition considered in this book, there are formal psychological and linguistic approaches now being developed. We heartily recommend you take advantage of some of these. Both before your departure and after you arrive in France, you will find experts in the multi-disciplined field of cultural transition which may be of great help.

L. Robert Kohls identifies four formal approaches to cross-cultural preparedness:
1. Education, which provides broad content knowledge of the subject country.
2. Training, which focuses on performing specific skills or meeting specific objectives effectively.
3. Orientation, which prepares a person to understand and function in another culture.
4. Briefing, which provides a broad overview of a culture.

Aspects of numbers 1, 3 and 4 are included elsewhere in this book and refer you to a number of resources, all included in the Bibliography. Many people are practising and developing number 2, cross-cultural training. An excellent source of both people and literature in this field is:

Society for International Educational Training And Research
733 15th St. NW Suite 900
Washington DC 20005
Tel: 202-296-4710

Membership is US$75 for Americans, US$60 for others. This fee includes scholarly quarterly journals, bi-monthly newsletters and networking services to other members and organizations. Book catalogs are available on request.

Another good source of inter-cultural training is:

BCIV Institute
American University
3301 New Mexico Ave NW
Washington DC 20016

Choosing an Inter-Cultural Trainer

We can only scratch the surface of the problem of cultural adaptation with this book. If you are planning to do business in France or coming to live in France for any reason, it would be well worth your while to get some intercultural training.

Kohls, again, offers some basic guidelines for choosing an international trainer who, he says, should have all the following qualifications:

1. Personal knowledge of France and at least two years of living experience there.
2. A positive attitude towards France and the French people.
3. The experience of having lived through culture shock, somewhere.
4. A fundamental knowledge of the basic values of your home culture.
5. Experience with stand-up training and experiential learning techniques.
6. Interest in both content and process training.
7. An image that is acceptable to the people he or she will be training.

Inter-cultural Trainers in Paris

In Paris, there are a number of experts in the field of cross-cultural communications. Here are a few of them:

- Franck Gauthey, tel: 48.04.09.47
- Kim Guptill, tel: 45.66.70.06
- Marie Lachze, tel: 34.80.08.38
- Dr. Paul Marcille (clinical psychologist), tel: 45.08.48.51
- Robert T. Moran, tel: 30.53.37.87
- Polly Plat, tel: 45.48.62.51
- Ann Williams-Gascon, tel: 48.28.03.21

LANGUAGE & CULTURE
Centers and Classes in France

No matter what your native culture, you are going to need help in France, and most sources for assistance here are open to everyone who speaks English. There are hundreds of them. Below we include a list of primary resources. These will lead you to the others.

CULTURAL RESOURCES IN ENGLISH, FRENCH AND ASIAN LANGUAGES IN FRANCE:

The American Chamber of Commerce
21 avenue George V, 75008 Paris; M: George V
Tel: 47.23.80.26

The American Church in Paris
Many programs and publications in addition to religious services, including "The Free Voice" monthly newspaper in English.
65 Quai D'Orsay, 75007 Paris; M: Invalides
Tel: 47.05.07.99

American Embassy
4 avenue Gabriel, 75008 Paris
Tel: 42.96.12.02

American Express
11 rue Scribe, 75009 Paris; M: Opéra
Tel: 42.66.09.99

The American Library in Paris
10, rue du Général Camou, 75007 Paris
Tel: 45.51.46.82
Open Tue – Sat, 14:00 – 19:00 hours

The American University of Paris
31 avenue Bosquet, 75007 Paris
Tel: 45.55.91.73
(The American University Bookstore is in the basement of the
American Church.)

The Association of American Wives of Europeans
49 rue Pierre Charoron, 75008 Paris
Tel: 42.56.05.24

Association pour la Diffusion de la Pensée Française
9 rue Anatole-de-la-forge
75017 Paris

Australian Embassy
4 rue Jean-Rey, 75015 Paris
Tel: 40.59.33.00

Bonne Journée
(This agency offers personalized services for individuals and small
groups)
6 place Charles-Dullin, 75018 Paris; M: Anvers
Tel: 46.06.24.17
Open Mon – Sat, 11:00 – 19:00 hours

Brentano's (English language bookstore)
37, avenue de l'Opéra, 75008 Paris; M: Opéra
Tel: 42.61.52.50

British and Commonwealth Women's Association
42 avenue Clodoald, 92210 St. Cloud
Tel: 47.71.17.93

The British Council
11 rue Constantine, 75007 Paris
Tel: 45.55.95.95

British Embassy
35 rue du Faubourg St. Honoré, 75008 Paris
Tel: 42.66.91.42

The British Institute in Paris
9 rue Constantine, 75007 Paris
Tel: 45.55.71.99

Canadian Embassy
35 avenue Montaigne, 75008 Paris
Tel: 47.23.01.01

Centre Culturel Canadien
5 rue Constantine, 75007 Paris
Tel: 45.51.35.73

France-USA Contacts
(Twice monthly classified advertisements in English)
19 rue Jean Beausire, 75004 Paris
Tel: 42.78.34.12
In New York: 228 E. 6th St., NYC. Tel: 212-777-3831

Franco-Indian Chamber of Commerce
4 avenue Daniel Lesueur, 75007 Paris
Tel: 43.06.88.97

Galerie Librarie Australienne (Books about Australia only)
7 rue Samson, St. Denis; M: Porte de Paris
Tel: 48.09.94.59
Open   Mon – Thurs, 14:00 – 19:00 hours
         Sat – Sun, 14:00 – 18:00 hours

Galignani (English language bookstore)
224 rue de Rivoli, 75001 Paris
Tel: 42.60.76.07

The General Store (food and things American)
82 rue de Grenelle, 75007 Paris
Tel: 45.48.63.16

Homelink
Delivers USA and UK publications in Paris
Tel: (16) 44.39.87.06

Indian Embassy
15 rue Alfred-Dehodencq, 75016 Paris
Tel: 45.20.39.30

Indonesian Embassy
49 rue Cortambert, 75016 Paris
Tel: 45.03.07.60

INSEAD (European Institute for Business Administration)
Boulevard de Constance
77305 Fontainbleau Cedex

Irish Embassy
4 rue Rude, 75116 Paris
Tel: 45.00.20.87

Japanese Embassy
7 avenue Hoche, 75008 Paris
Tel: 47.66.02.22

Japon Service Culturel
7 rue de Tilsitt, 75017 Paris
Tel: 47.66.02.22

Korean Cultural Center
2 avenue d'Iena, 75016 Paris
Tel: 47.20.83.86

Malaysian Embassy
32 rue Spontini, 75016 Paris
Tel: 45.53.11.85

New Zealand Embassy
7 ter rue L. deVinci, 75116 Paris
Tel: 45.00.24.11

Pakistan Embassy
18 rue Lord-Byron, 75008 Paris
Tel: 45.62.23.32

People's Republic of China Embassy
21 rue Am d'Estaing, 75016 Paris
Tel: 47.23.32.90

PRC-Cultural Services
9 avenue Victor-Cresson, Issy-les Moulineaux
Tel: 47.36.77.04

Philippine Embassy
39 avenue Georges Mandel, 75116 Paris
Tel: 47.04.65.50

The Paris Traveler's Gazette
Carrefour des Etats-Unis, 5 Place André Malraux, 75001 Paris
Tel: 42.60.32.52

St. Michael's Church (Anglican)
5 rue d'Aguesseau, 75008 Paris
Tel: 47.42.70.88

Shakespeare & Co.
37 rue de la Bucherie, 75005 Paris; M: St. Michel

SIETAR
Society for International Educational Training And Research
122, avenue Nollet, 75017 Paris; M: Brochant
Tel: 52.26.63.13

Singapore Embassy
12 avenue Square Foch, 75116 Paris
Tel: 45.00.33.61

South Korean Embassy
125 rue de Grenelle, 75007 Paris
Tel: 47.53.01.01

Sri Lankan Embassy
15 rue d'Astorg, 75008 Paris
Tel: 42.66.35.01

Taiwan Embassy
Aspect, 9 avenue Matignon, 75008 Paris
Tel: 42.99.16.80

Thailand Embassy
8 rue Greuze, 75116 Paris
Tel: 47.04.32.22

The Village Voice Bookstore
6 rue Princesse, 75006 Paris; M: Mabillon

W.H. Smith & Son (English Language Bookstore)
248 rue de Rivoli, 75002 Paris
Tel: 42.60.37.97

Women's Institute for Continuing Education (WICE)
(part of the American University in Paris)
Courses and programs for English-speaking people in France
20 boulevard Montparnasse, 75015 Paris; M: Duroc
Tel: 45.66.75.50
Open Mon – Fri, 09:00 – 17:00 hours

FRENCH LANGUAGE SCHOOLS IN FRANCE
In addition to some of the sources above, here are the best-known
schools for teaching French in Paris:
Alliance Française
101 boulevard Raspail, 75006 Paris
Tel: 45.44.38.28
Information: 34 rue de Fleurus

Berlitz has six schools in Paris and four in the suburbs.
Good, but expensive.
35 avenue Franklin Roosevelt, 75008 Paris
Tel: 47.20.41.60

Cours de Civilisation et Langue Française de la Sorbonne
47 rue des Ecoles, 75007 Paris
Tel: 43.29.12.13
(A-levels or High School diploma required)

Institut Catholique de Paris
21 rue d'Assas, 75006 Paris
Tel: 42.22.41.80

CAN YOU GO HOME AGAIN?

Experienced cross-culturalists will tell you that the hardest part of the international experience is usually the return home. Though you can never totally integrate into another culture, you may well find re-integrating into your first culture the most difficult transition of all. Nobody has studied the problem long enough to explain why.

It is clear that we adapt to other cultures in both conscious and subconscious ways. Re-adapting to our former cultural "norm" takes by far the most conscious effort.

Even if you conscientiously resist another culture, you will still pick up habits and amend old patterns, inspite of yourself. We human beings can't help being conformists; our subconscious conforms for us, even if we don't. This is not a new phenomenon. History and literature provide many such examples.

The impressions of living in a different culture are not really reversible. Going home is another complex cultural transition, a new relationship to an old cultural setting, one where you don't expect to have trouble. Expect this part of your international experience to take from six months to a year.

I have met many people doing business internationally who find going home the most difficult transition of all. They call it a kind of reverse homesickness. This lends strength to the argument that the closer a culture is to your own, the more difficult it will be to adjust to. The depth of shock, or pain, is not related to the depth of cultural understanding, but to the cultural expectations not met or not recognized. France ought to be an easy adjustment, and it isn't. Going home ought to be easy, and it isn't.

The problems of going home are several. You don't know what has gone on there. You are out of touch with local news and gossip.

Your old friends will not understand or recognize the changes you have made in your values and habits. They will be quickly bored by tales of your life abroad, even though they will express interest. Their lives revolve around a different center.

Your explanations of how you lived and what you did will quickly be judged as "bragging". That description of the French cuisine you enjoyed is not appropriate at the barbeque your friends have prepared for your return. Slides of the beautiful countryside of Burgundy will fail to impress your old buddy who never tasted the 1983 vintage. Try to keep to frames of reference that will work fòr your old friends.

Likewise, any complaints about how difficult things were will be taken very lightly:

"You were lonely in Paris? Are you kidding?"

"What do you mean the Paris office is very formal? They seem quite relaxed when I visit."

"What in the world is the matter with you? You used to love these hamburgers."

You have changed, sometimes in ways you didn't even know. This will intimidate your friends, and you, yourself. Just be prepared for it and give yourself and your friends the patience and understanding you have learned to use abroad.

At the Home Office

Your company will be one in a thousand if it expresses any interest in the "expertise" you've gained in working in the French branch. They figure the French locals are the experts. You were just a go-between. You're back; the job's done. The next person assigned to Paris will be left to go through all the painful learning experiences you did. And the bridges you painstakingly built between yourself and the Paris staff will be invisible to your boss.

This, we hope, is changing. Companies are starting to develop sensitivities to the invisible aspects of international relations. They are beginning to recognize that language is not enough, that the synergy of business relations requires deep inter-cultural understanding. More and more, internationals, like yourself, will be called upon to make the different applications of company policy work. The heterogeneous aspect of international life is a source of richness, if used properly, as Franck Gauthey et. al. have said.

The expanded view of one's universe that the international life gives also makes certain aspects of one's own culture less palatable, less satisfying. But such expansion is essential, in international living and international relations. Keep struggling with your own cultural transitions and don't give up hope. The world cannot afford to kill the messenger.

BIBLIOGRAPHY AND RECOMMENDED READING

"There is help for those who wish it. Those who say they don't need it may be too blind to recognize the problem. The irony is that they need the help most of all."

—Robert T. Moran

The field of cross-cultural understanding mixes all the disciplines. Everything you read about France and about the problems of cultural transition will help. Our short bibliography and recommended reading list is broken up into various approaches to the people and the problem of culture shock in France. It is just to get you started and is by no means complete.

The French Today

"A Little Tour Through France" by Henry James is considered a classic now.

"The French" by Theodore Zeldin, 1986. Pantheon.

"An American in Paris" by Genet (Janet Flanner); also "Men and Monuments" originally published by "The New Yorker" magazine.

"Darlinghissima: Letters to a Friend" by Janet Flanner, edited by

Natalia Danesi Murray. Harcourt, Brace Jovanovich, New York. 1985.

"Is Socialism Doomed? The Meaning of Mitterrand" by Daniel Singer. Oxford University Press. 1988.

"Population and Society in Twentieth Century France" by Colin Dyer. Holmes & Meier Publishers Inc., New York. 1978.

"The Europeans" by Luigi Barzini. Simon & Schuster, New York. 1983.

"Europeans" by Jane Kramer. Farrar, Straus & Giroux, New York. 1988.

"The People of Paris" by Joseph Barry. Doubleday & Co., New York. 1966.

"The Rules of the Game" by Nathan Leites. Translated by Derek Coltman. University of Chicago Press. 1969.

"French Regional Cooking" by Anne Willan. Hutchinson & Co. (Publishers) Ltd., London. Marshall paperback edition. 1983.

"The French at Table" by Rudolph Chelminski. William Morrow and Company Inc., New York. 1985.

"A Food Lover's Guide to France" by Patricia Wells, 1988. Workman, New York. Also her "Food Lover's Guide to Paris", both of them excellent restaurant and food guides, approaching the subject of eating from any number of perspectives.

"Paris La Nuit Sexy" 20th edition, 1989. Editions Edicart's SARL, 63 rue de la Prévoyance, 94300 Vincennes. Tel: 43.65.73.70.

"The Identity of France" by Fernand Braudel. Translated by Sian Reynolds. Collins, Harper & Row. 1988.

"France Today" by John Ardagh. Penguin. 1988.

"The French Through Their Films" by Robin Buss. Unger, 1988.

How-to Help for Internationals in France

"Do's and Taboos around the World" compiled by the Parker Pen Company. The Benjamin Company, Elmsford, New York. 1985.

"Cultural Misunderstandings: The French-American Experience" by

Raymonde Carroll. Translated by Carol Volk. The University of Chicago Press. 1988. (Orig. "Evidences invisbles" by Editions du Seuil, 1987.)

"Coping with France" by Fay Sharman. Basil Blackwell Inc., London and New York. 1987.

"Bloom Where You're Planted" by the Women of the American Church in Paris. 1988. Paris.

"Health Care Resources in Paris", published by the Community Health Care Committee of the Women's Institute for Continuing Education at the American College in Paris. 1985. (Revised in 1989.)

"Guide to Education", compiled and edited by Anita Tassel and Carolyn White-Lesieur. Published by the Association of American Wives of Europeans, Paris. 1987.

"The Transplanted Woman" by Gabrielle Varro. A Study of French-American Marriages in France. Praeger, Westport CT. 1988.

"How-to Europe" by John Bermont. Murphy & Broad, Newport Beach, CA. 1986

"European Customs & Manners" by Nancy L. Braganti and Elizabeth Devine. Meadowbrook Inc., Deephaven MN. 1984.

"When in France" by C. Sinclair-Stevenson. Touchstone Books. 1989.

"France: What to Know & Expect", by Betty Springer. Peanut Butter, USA. 1988.

French History and Literature

"Les Grands Auteurs Français du Programme" by André Lagarde and Laurent Michard. Les Editions Bordas in Paris. A summary series of French literature, by century, in French.

"Diderot: The Virtue of a Philosopher" by Carol Blum. The Viking Press. 1974.

"Richelieu and the French Monarchy" by C.V. Wedgewood. Collier Books, New York. 1962.

"The Marquis de Sade" by Geofrey Gorer. Liveright Publishing

Corp., New York. 1934.

"Napoleon III and the Rebuilding of Paris" by David H. Pinkney. Princeton University Press. 1958.

"Candide" by Voltaire (François Marie Arouet). 1759. A philosophical novel, examining life's difficulties and evils at the time of the Enlightenment in France, and calling for action. The time we give to something makes it important, Voltaire said, so it is wise to judge carefully how we give our time.

"Les Misérables" by Victor Hugo. 1862. A social novel conveying simple, humanistic ideals.

"The Ethics of Ambiguity" by Simone deBeauvoir, lifelong companion of Jean Paul Sartre, the great 20th century existentialist. The two of them believed that man's life is totally his own responsibilty, though he tries to absolve that by creating other forces and causes, such as religion.

"The Little Prince" by Antoine de Saint-Exupéry, also in the 1930s, found popularity all over the world, espousing the French concept of the nobility of man which began with Voltaire.

"Antigone", "Becket", "The Rehearsal", or any of the other plays of Jean Anouilh, the world's most performed playwright today.

The French Language

"Merde!" and "Merde Encore!" by Genevieve, Angus & Robertson.

"Street French" by David Burke, John Wiley & Sons.

"Conversational French in 20 Lessons", the Cortina Method. R.D. Cortina Co. Inc., New York. 1977.

Culture Shock in General

"Culture Shock: Psychological Reactions to Unfamiliar Environments" by Adrian Furnham and Stephen Bochner. Methuen & Co. Ltd, London. 1986. Good bibliography on the subject.

"Cultures in Contact: Studies in Cross-Cultural Interaction", edited by Stephen Bochner. Pergamon Press Ltd. 1982.

"Intercultural Training: Don't Leave Home Without It" by Robert Kohls. SIETAR International, Washington DC. 1984.

"Training for the Multicultural Manager" and "Training for the Cross-Cultural Mind" by Pierre Casse, SIETAR, Washington DC. 1984.

"Managing Cultural Differences" by Philip R. Harris and Robert T. Moran. Gulf Publishing Co., Houston, Texas, USA. Revised 1987.

"Leaders Sans Frontières" by Franck Gauthey et. al., McGraw-Hill, Paris. 1988.

"International Management", a monthly magazine published by McGraw-Hill House, Maidenhead, SL6 2QL Berkshire, England. Tel: (0628) 23431.

"Language Contact and Bilingualism" by René Appel & Pieter Muysken. Edward Arnold, London. 1987.

"Acts of Identity" by R. le Page and A. Tabouret-Keller. Cambridge University Press. 1985.

"Venturing Abroad: Europe" by Robert T. Moran. International Management/McGraw-Hill, London. 1989.

"The Hidden Dimension", "The Silent Language" and "Beyond Culture" by Edward T. Hall. Anchor Press, Doubleday. 1977.

General Guides

MAPS: Michelin Green Guide Series and Institut Géographique National.

"France", Michelin. 1989

"French Farm & Village Holiday Guide", Hunter Publications, New York. 1989

"The Best of France", Gault Millau. Prentice-Hall. 1989

CULTURAL QUIZ
Situation 1

An evening at a good French restaurant is planned with friends visiting Paris. You've made reservations and arrive a bit late to find the maître d' cool and the waiters unfriendly. Your guests complain that French people are rude. Do you:

A. Agree with your friends and concede that this is just another example, making a good evening inspite of it by laughing with your friends at the supercilious attitude of the staff?

B. Ignore your friends' comment and apologise for being late and strive all evening to make up for it to the restaurant staff?

C. Interpret the attitude at the restaurant as normal and brush off your friends' comments?

D. Strive to explain to your friends about the Paris waiter's rudeness game and show them how to play it, in return?

E. Attempt through your serious interest in the wine and cuisine to win over the waiters and prove your friends wrong?

225

Comments

This situation crops up so many times in Paris, it should be in every guidebook. French waiters are professionals, they take their work seriously and with pride. By recognizing them as professionals you can avoid the emotional reaction of feeling rejected by their coolness, and teach your compatriots to take the French attitude towards food. So, option E is the most productive, though you can still enjoy your evening with your friends by ignoring the situation, which makes you appear rude, in turn, to the restaurant staff and reconfirms their view that foreigners don't appreciate French cuisine.

Situation 2

You've just moved into your apartment and you need to order telephone service/plumbing repairs/electrical service. Do you...

A. Call the company and try to make arrangements over the telephone?

B. Visit your nearest Telecom office, plumber or EGF shop and ask them for the service you need, in person?

C. Contact the *gardienne* or *concierge* in your building and ask them to handle the job for you, expecting to pay a handsome tip?

D. Ask your secretary at work to handle these details?

Comments

In France, people tend to do their own chores, and there is little crossover between personal and private life. Your secretary will not expect to have such private matters in her hands. Although the *gardienne* in your building could help you with some details of private life, you will find that things happen most expediently when you go, in person, to the office or service company you require. It is usually more difficult to get anything like services, train reservations and specific information accomplished over the telephone. Projects such as the telephone service installation will take some time, standing in lines, filling out forms and showing identification. Take along all your documents and have all your questions ready in advance. Remember, only your specific questions will be answered and few helpful suggestions will be volunteered. Treat the person helping you as you would treat a stranger giving requested assistance. Expect less than enthusiastic response to your dilemma. Take some reading material, to occupy your time while waiting. Be patient.

Situation 3

You have just arrived at the company offices where you will be working in Paris. You have already met most of your fellow workers on previous visits. Now you are coming in as a "local" staff member, yourself. A group at the office are going to lunch and invite you to join them, but once at the restaurant the conversation turns to politics, and a roaring argument develops, in French. Your reaction is:

A. To sit in shock, unable to eat, fearing physical violence will erupt at any moment.

B. Realize that your new French friends have turned their back on you, speaking quickly in French to one another without regard for your limited language skills. Assume you are an outsider and expected to sit quietly by while they discuss the details of their own political situation.

C. Vow to improve your language skills so that you can participate, and follow the conversation closely.

D. Make your comments, if you understand the gist of the conversation, even if you can only express yourself in English, when there is a lull in the conversation and you see a chance to jump in without interrupting.

E. Scold the group for being far too heated on the subject of politics and try to turn the conversation back to English and to matters of business that are on your mind.

Comments

Many French people love to discuss and debate, especially on the subject of politics. Debate, itself, is an art form in France, and their English skills may not be sufficient for such parrying. So resign yourself to listening to frequent heated debates in French, during the lunch hour, especially on the subject of politics. Your growing skills in the language, and growing knowledge of French politics, will make these experiences more interesting, and soon you will be able to take part in the conversation. They are a vital part of living in France.

Situation 4

You are invited to dinner with French acquaintances. It is for 20:00 hours and you arrive early to an elegant apartment, with a bottle of white wine which needs chilling. You offer to put the bottle in the refrigerator and ask where the kitchen is. Your hostess takes the wine, leads you to the living room instead, and keeps you there until dinner is served in the dining room. After the meal, you depart the same way you came in, feeling you've been treated as a stranger and not as a friend. You wanted to see the whole apartment! Do you

A. Assume that you have been given the "cold shoulder" and refuse their next invitation as insincere?

B. Confront your acquaintances on your discomfort and ask them what you did "wrong", but find they don't seem to understand your question?

C. Feel distanced from these people but reciprocate your hosts' efforts, nonetheless, with a dinner at your favorite restaurant? In that environment, they appear to be more open and friendly.

D. Return to your hosts' home and expect, this time, to be entertained only in the living room and dining room, recognizing that your presence in the house is already a display of intimacy, even if the rest of the house if off limits?

E. Confront your hosts in the first place and ask to see the house when you first arrive?

229

Comments

The French do not make a habit of "showing off" their house to first-time guests. It would be considered boastful on their part. So if you really want to see the house, ask in advance of your arrival, to give them time to prepare it for you properly. Otherwise, if you are not invited to take a look around it, don't ask yourself into any room that is not shown to you (except of course the toilet, which you can ask for!). Don't take this modesty as a lack of intimacy.

Situation 5

You are on the street looking for a certain gourmet food shop you thought was on that block but isn't. Your time is short and you've left the address at home. You ask which of the following people for help:

A. A policeman ambling down the street?

B. A businessman with a briefcase briskly walking the same way?

C. An older woman in black bent over and moving slowly towards the *métro*?

D. The *métro* ticket seller?

E. A fashionable, well-dressed woman of middle age waiting for the light?

Comments

Choosing the person from whom you ask directions in France is very important, when seeking a good answer. Unless your question involves traffic law, don't seek the help of a policeman, or anyone else in uniform. They do not consider it their job to direct either locals or foreigners, and they often do not speak another language. The same with the *métro* ticket seller. Giving directions is not part of their job. A person with a brisk walk may well be in a hurry, best not to interrupt him, as a proper explanation may take some time and patience he isn't able to give. Finally, an older woman in black is probably from the countryside, may not know the area well, and certainly wouldn't be frequenting gourmet food stores. It's best to choose the person most likely to know the shop and least preoccupied with other duties.

Situation 6

You are included in your first business meeting at work. Your boss acts as chairperson and he requests progress reports on a specific project from various members of your teams dealing with different aspects of the job. To your surprise, as each person's turn comes, he or she seems full of complaints and problems to report, often turning blame for the situation on your boss. Your turn comes. Do you

A. Take the same pose, presenting your situation as too difficult and demanding help from your boss?
B. Pass, leaving your report unsaid?
C. Give the report you had planned to give, outlining the current situation but without any criticism or complaint?
D. Turn to other members of the group whom you feel have unfairly criticized the boss and explain your criticism?
E. Assume that your boss is just about to be fired and you'll be looking for another job tomorrow?

Comments

Meetings in France have a function similar to luncheon discussions. Members participating are expected to be critical and discriminating in their observations. Although they may appear to be putting blame on the chairman's head, such comments are more an opportunity for the speaker to exhibit his command and skill in his job. The chairman will not take honest criticism personally, but he will listen critically, as all others in the room are expected to do. So, it will not be your job to defend your boss. He does not feel threatened. It will be your job, however, to sharpen up your report to convey your own skills at discerning both negative and positive aspects of your particular situation. A sweetened version of the facts will not impress the boss or impress him with your skills. It will be taken badly, as a false compliment. Better to prepare a sharp, observant report in advance.

Situation 7

You have established certain shops in your neighborhood as your regular stops. One day, when you are in a hurry with a long shopping list, the lady who sells you cheeses begins a long explanation of the day's specials and then begins a story about a pickpocket who was apprehended by an angry victim on the street corner the previous day. You can see the story is going to take some time and you don't want to be held up indefinitely. Do you

A. Interrupt the speaker, explain that you are in a hurry, and ask for your bill?

B. Let her finish her story and then express regret, followed immediately by "How much do I owe you?"

C. Console the lady about the growing violence on the streets and confirm that active victims get better results than the police force, then say you will return for your packages later?

Comments

Relationships, both in business and personal life, are critical in France and being in a hurry is hardly considered sufficient grounds for denying your acquaintances the chance to express their concerns and convey exciting neighborhood gossip. People you do business with regularly, especially those shopkeepers in your neighborhood who recognize you as a regular, will make a special effort with you, as a valued customer. Such conversation is one of the ways they establish that intimacy and give special treatment. By brushing them aside, you destroy the delicate bridge of friendship that they are building. However, we all get in a hurry at times, so by apologizing for your hurry and making a special effort with that shopkeeper the next time you are buying, you can avoid damage to the relationship.

DO'S AND DONT'S

- DO use *Madame*, *Monsieur* and *Mademoiselle* when saying hello and goodbye, along with a hand-shake.
- DON'T use first names, or even last names, unless the person also knows and uses your first and last name.
- DON'T give prices of things you have bought.
- DON'T ask what someone does for a living or how much money he makes.
- DO ask a French person who he voted for in the election.
- DON'T ask about a person's family or a person's age unless you are on intimate terms and he has asked you similar questions, already.
- DO return a compliment or praise with an expression of admiration for that person's judgement.
- DON'T speak or laugh loudly in public places.
- DO say *Bonjour* and *Merci* on entering and leaving a shop.
- DO dress sharply, to the French expectation.
- DON'T open a closed door without knocking first. But DON'T wait for a reply before entering. A knock means "I'm coming in", in France.
- DON'T follow your host around the house, in a French home. Stay out of the kitchen and don't even pour yourself a drink, unless invited to do so.

- DO watch carefully, in conversation, for signs of boredom, or the desire of your listener to speak. Be ready to change the topic at any time.
- DON'T respond to catcalls of construction workers and strangers on the street.
- DO respond to the comments of the shopkeepers.

THE AUTHOR

Sally Taylor is the product of two distinct American cultures: her father was a Yankee, her mother a Confederate. Though the War between the States was over before her respective grandparents were born, she grew up in Baltimore, halfway between her parents' homes, and learned early that at least part of "reality" is a question of cultural perspective.

Thus she took readily to journalism and, in her university days in the late 1960s, served as managing editor at the Boston University News. Upon graduation, she spent a year vagabonding through Europe and North Africa and decided to dedicate her life to journalism and the multi-cultural life.

In the late 1970s, she lived in California, moving up the job ladder fron reporter to editor to publisher. Her home base is still a Victorian cottage in San Francisco, from which she publishes bicycle tours of the wine country (for both California and France) under the imprint *Sally Taylor & Friends*, but she prefers the role of reporter.

She has spent the last ten years working as a foreign correspondent in Asia and in Europe, and keeps pieds-à-terre in Hong Kong and Paris. She has written for a wide range of publications including *The Asian Wall Street Journal*, *The International Herald Tribune* and *Publishers Weekly*.

INDEX